"Despite that fact that, in recent years, muc New Testament's most difficult book to un an important theme of the sermon, its spiri McCruden, an accomplished commentator on Hebrews, has turned his attention to this aspect of Hebrews and has presented a clear, coherent, and compelling study of its spirituality. His presentation of Christian spirituality as a commitment to the transcendent presence of God in the life, death, and resurrection of Jesus Christ establishes the basis for the religious experience of the recipients of Hebrews as fundamentally Christocentric. Considering also the very real concerns and sufferings of the actual Hebrews' community, McCruden shows how the author of Hebrews presents Jesus as a model of the perfect response to God in perseverance and obedience, to offer encouragement and incentive to his audience. Jesus' own pilgrimage from the mundane to the eternal establishes a pattern to be emulated by the recipients of Hebrews, on their own pilgrimage toward God. In this way, the spirituality of Hebrews is also communal as it enriches the life of an ecclesial community accessing God though Christ in the midst of the challenges of daily living. Opening up a much-needed area of the study of Hebrews, McCruden's work will benefit a wide audience ranging from scholars dedicated to the study of Hebrews to students eager to discover what Hebrews has to offer them."

— Alan C. Mitchell
    Associate Professor of New Testament and
        Christian Origins
    Director, The Annual Georgetown University
        Institute on Sacred Scripture
    Georgetown University
    Washington, DC

"Prof. McCruden's careful reading of Hebrews yields a persuasive religious interpretation of the letter that is both constrained and richly informed by historical criticism. 'Spirituality,' defined as the intersection of the transcendent with the concrete circumstances of the letter's readers, finds its focus in Christ not merely because he is 'God with us' but primarily because Jesus' path to perfection includes his earthly life of obedience, suffering, and death, as well as his exaltation to the transcendent heavenly sanctuary. Thus, the spirituality of Hebrews, understood in corporate terms, depends on the paradigmatic and exemplary role of Jesus and is meant to guide his followers in their present journey along the path to the transcendent goal Jesus has already attained."

— Rowan A. Greer
    Professor Emeritus
    Yale Divinity School

"Many scholars have examined the theology of Hebrews, but Kevin McCruden has done what few have attempted. He has teased out the spirituality of one of the most engaging books of the New Testament. Clearly written and always in conversation with the best of contemporary scholarship, McCruden's study challenges scholars to view Hebrews from a new vantage point. Most important, by bridging the gap between theology and spirituality, this work provides all of us with an engaging way to understand our lives as Christians today."

> — Frank J. Matera
> Pastor, St. Mary's Church
> Simsbury, Connecticut
> Author, *The Sermon on the Mount*

"Illuminating the faithfulness displayed during the human experience of Jesus, McCruden introduces major issues in the field of Hebrews' study as he sets them in the applicable context of the letter's spirituality. Insightful treatments on topics such as prayer and the speaking blood of Abel contribute to a call to follow the sermon's countercultural exhortation to faithfulness. I will recommend this text for those just beginning to study Hebrews, even as I plan to use it on my own continuing work on the epistle."

> — Amy Peeler
> Assistant Professor of New Testament
> Wheaton College

"Kevin B. McCruden brings a scholarly mind and a pastoral heart to this volume. The result is an accessible, engaging exposition of the theological message of the Epistle to the Hebrews that is grounded in an expert's understanding of the text and its ancient setting. McCruden especially shines when addressing the epistle's discussion of suffering."

> — Eric F. Mason
> Professor of Biblical Studies
> Judson University

A Body You Have Prepared for Me

The Spirituality of the
Letter to the Hebrews

Kevin B. McCruden

A Michael Glazier Book

LITURGICAL PRESS

Collegeville, Minnesota

www.litpress.org

A Michael Glazier Book published by Liturgical Press

Cover design by Jodi Hendrickson. Sacrifice of Abel and Melchizedek. Mosaic in Basilica of San Vitale in Ravenna. Photo courtesy of Wikimedia Commons.

1   2   3   4   5   6   7   8   9

Library of Congress Cataloging-in-Publication Data

McCruden, Kevin B.
    A body you have prepared for me : the spirituality of the Letter to the Hebrews / Kevin B. McCruden.
        pages   cm
    "A Michael Glazier book."
    Includes bibliographical references and index.
    ISBN 978-0-8146-5888-8 (pbk. : alk. paper) —
    ISBN 978-0-8146-8211-1 (e-book)
    1. Bible. Hebrews—Criticism, interpretation, etc.   I. Title.

    BS2775.52.M335   2013
    227'.8706—dc23

                                                                            2013007671

Contents

Abbreviations

AB	Anchor Bible
Bib	*Biblica*
BR	*Biblical Research*
BSac	*Bibliotheca Sacra*
BZNW	*Beihefte zur Zeitschrift für die neutestamentliche Wissenschaft*
CBQ	*Catholic Biblical Quarterly*
CBQMS	Catholic Biblical Quarterly Monograph Series
HNTC	Harper's New Testament Commentaries
HTR	*Harvard Theological Review*
HNT	Handbuch zum Neuen Testament
JBL	*Journal of Biblical Literature*
JSNTSup	*Journal for the Study of the New Testament: Supplement Series*
NICNT	New International Commentary on the New Testament
NIGTC	New International Greek Testament Commentary
NovTSup	Supplements to Novum Testamentum
NRSV	New Revised Standard Version
NTOA	Novum Testamentum et Orbis Antiquus
PRSt	*Perspectives in Religious Studies*
RevExp	*Review and Expositor*
SBLDS	Society of Biblical Literature Dissertation Series
SBLRBS	Society of Biblical Literature Resources for Biblical Study
SNTSMS	Society for New Testament Studies Monograph Series
SP	Sacra Pagina

SR	*Studies in Religion*
TJ	*Trinity Journal*
TynBul	*Tyndale Bulletin*
WBC	Word Biblical Commentary
WUNT	Wissenshaftliche Untersuchungen zum Neuen Testament

Preface

This exploration into the understanding of spirituality articulated in the Letter to the Hebrews stems from my continued fascination with the complex Christology of this early Christian homily. Few texts from the New Testament combine with such a masterful equilibrium a depiction of Christ as a heavenly figure and the historical memory of the human Jesus who endured testing and abuse for the sake of embodying God's kingdom of self-sacrificial justice. Perhaps even fewer texts offer a more challenging read for the contemporary reader. To give just one example: while the ancient audience of Hebrews would have recognized as perfectly obvious the author's frequent association of religiosity with the language of temples, sacrifice, and priests and high priests, this same language can make the appropriation of Hebrews a daunting enterprise for many readers today.

Although it is important not to minimize the challenges inherent to reading a text as complex as Hebrews, I wish to suggest that this letter more than rewards an attentive reading of its distinctive understanding of Christ as an eternal high priest. If it is true, as I would maintain it is, that the generative source of the varied writings we encounter in the New Testament resides in the realm of deeply personal religious experience, then Hebrews affords us a truly exquisite example of a particularly creative interpretation of such religious experience. Hebrews also supplies us with something all too rare in many of the documents of the New Testament: a glimpse into the personal experiences of the ancient persons who first heard this text. Partially obscured beneath the author's characteristic emphasis on the superiority of transcendent realities is the indelible imprint of the real life experiences of early Christians who suffered emotionally and physically for the countercultural commitment that they placed in Jesus. For such persons, Hebrews vividly celebrates the unseen vindication of Jesus and, in this way, provides a hope-filled portrait of the victorious Son of God. At the same time, Hebrews is also very much concerned with what we might call the life of Christian discipleship—that is, what it means to journey this side of the age to come in a manner that is faithful to the countercultural character of God's kingdom embodied by Jesus. It is my hope that this brief study will help illumine for the reader something of this creative balance between the transcendent and the concrete that Hebrews illustrates so well.

Now that this project is complete, I would like to take this opportunity to thank those whose generous assistance has contributed to the successful completion of this book. The early stages of writing were aided greatly by a sabbatical leave granted by Gonzaga University for which I am most grateful. In addition, several of my colleagues from the religious studies department at Gonzaga University generously read through various editions of the chapters. I would like especially to thank both Joy Milos and Ron Large for their helpful comments, particularly with regard to the organization of the opening chapter. A special word of thanks goes to Alan C. Mitchell of Georgetown University, who provided both valuable editorial assistance and generous encouragement throughout the entire project. I would also like to thank both the Society of Biblical Literature and the *Catholic Biblical Quarterly* for their kind permission to use previously published material for this book. Brief portions from Kevin B. McCruden, "The Concept of Perfection in the Epistle to the Hebrews," *Reading the Epistle to the Hebrews: A Resource for Students*, Society of Biblical Literature Resources for Biblical Study 66, ed. Eric F. Mason and Kevin B. McCruden (Atlanta: Society of Biblical Literature, 2011): 209–29, appear in chapters 2 and 3; and chapter 4 represents an adapted version of Kevin B. McCruden, "The Eloquent Blood of Jesus: The Neglected Theme of the Fidelity of Jesus in Hebrews 12:24," *Catholic Biblical Quarterly* 75 (2013): 504–20. Finally, I want to express my perpetual gratitude to my wife Kerry and our young sons Liam and Sam. In the course of this book coming to fruition they graciously endured the long absences of a husband and dad. This book is dedicated to them and they deserve my full attention now.

Defining Spirituality

Spirituality is a concept that resists precise definition. The appendix of a recent study on Christian spirituality, for example, offers for the consideration of the reader no less than twenty-three definitions of the term.[1] For some, spirituality amounts to little more than an alternative expression for an active prayer life, while for others the concept carries the connotation of the therapeutic.[2] For still others, spirituality is synonymous with a contemplative emphasis on the interior life or even a rather inchoate focus on personal piety in general. No doubt the concept of spirituality implies for many some sort of relationship with, or thinking about, God. However, it is not requisite that spirituality must have an explicitly religious character to count as authentically spiritual. If, as Karl Rahner famously articulated, human beings have the capacity to transcend themselves through the pursuit of knowledge, freedom, and love, then the concept of spirituality can encompass something at once as ordinary yet sublime as the experience of falling in love, or losing oneself in the practice of a vocation.[3] Hence, spirituality can be theocentric, but it need not be and still count as authentically spiritual.

---

[1] See Lawrence S. Cunningham and Keith J. Egan, *Christian Spirituality: Themes from the Tradition* (New Jersey: Paulist Press, 1996), 22–28.

[2] See Patrick J. Hartin, *Exploring the Spirituality of the Gospels* (Collegeville, MN: Liturgical Press, 2010), 1–2.

[3] See Michael Downey's helpful assessment of the anthropological reflections of Karl Rahner in *Understanding Christian Spirituality* (New Jersey: Paulist Press, 1997), 32–35.

A specifically Christian spirituality, however, is self-consciously religious in character and decidedly theocentric for at least two reasons. First, by its very definition, Christian spirituality is committed to a perception of the transcendent presence of God as revealed in the life, death, and resurrection of Jesus Christ. By virtue of the response of faith, Christians perceive Jesus of Nazareth to be Emmanuel or "God is with us" (Matt 1:23). Likewise, Christians confess this same Jesus to be the Son of God who, in his status as the exalted Son, promises to remain forever with the faithful even to the close of the age (Matt 28:20). For such persons, Jesus is a divine presence whom they personally and powerfully encounter in their lives.

Those who profess themselves to be Christians attest, in other words, to an encounter with God that they believe to be mediated through the person of Jesus Christ as received by the Spirit. While this conviction is more or less explicit in nearly every book of the New Testament, the apostle Paul gives especially eloquent expression to this faith commitment when he declares in 2 Corinthians 4:6: "For it is the God who said, 'Let light shine out of darkness,' who has shone in our hearts to give the light of the knowledge of the glory of God in the face of Jesus Christ."[4] The majestic opening line of the Letter to the Hebrews makes much the same point by applying the metaphor of speech to God: "Long ago God spoke to our ancestors in many and various ways by the prophets, but in these last days he has spoken to us by a Son" (Heb 1:1). Second, Christian spirituality necessarily privileges what it takes to be the revelatory witness of Scripture to attest to this fundamental, transcendental claim. While originally mediated by the historically and theologically diverse writings that comprise the New Testament, the primitive Christian experience of having encountered God in the person of Jesus can be actualized again and again down to the present day. This insight is given clear expression in the Gospel According to John: "Now Jesus did many other signs in the presence of his disciples, which are not written in this book. But these

---

[4] All Scripture is from the NRSV unless otherwise specified. Unless indicated otherwise, all other translations from ancient sources are taken from the Loeb Classical Library.

are written so that you may come to believe that Jesus is the Messiah, the Son of God, and that through believing you may have life in his name" (John 20:30-31). Since the origins of the Latin term *spiritualitas* derive from later Christian reflection on the correspondence of the apostle Paul, the writings of the self-described *apostle to the Gentiles* represent an appropriate entry point into our initial analysis of the topic of Christian spirituality.[5]

Distressed upon hearing reports of competitive rivalries proliferating within the Corinthian community, Paul chides the Corinthian Christians in the following manner:

> And so, brothers and sisters, I could not speak to you as spiritual people [*pneumatikois*], but rather as people of the flesh [*sarkinois*], as infants in Christ. . . . Even now you are still not ready, for you are still of the flesh [*sarkikoi*]. For as long as there is jealousy and quarreling among you, are you not of the flesh [*sarkikoi*], and behaving according to human inclinations? For when one says, "I belong to Paul," and another, "I belong to Apollos," are you not merely human? (1 Cor 3:1-3)

The presenting issue illustrated by this passage involves the interpersonal conduct of the communities under Paul's apostolic guidance. An especially helpful principle to keep in mind when reading Paul's letters is that Paul was less a theologian than he was a practical pastor; as such, the principal aim of much of his correspondence was to shape his congregants into certain kinds of persons—namely, communities characterized by holiness and countercultural living.[6] Paul believed that when followers became incorporated into Christ through the response of faith and the ritual act of baptism, a transfer of sorts occurred; in some mysterious, but very real sense, believers began to participate in Christ.[7] While such participation did not entail any sort of notion of a

---

[5] See Philip Sheldrake, *A Brief History of Spirituality* (London: Wiley-Blackwell, 2007), 23.

[6] It is certain at the very least that Paul should not be understood as a systematic theologian. See Jouette M. Bassler, *Navigating Paul: An Introduction to Key Theological Concepts* (Louisville: Westminster John Knox, 2007), ix.

[7] See Leander E. Keck, *Paul and His Letters*, 2nd ed. (Philadelphia: Fortress Press, 1988), 56.

departure from earthly existence according to Paul, it did mean that believers were no longer to think of themselves as strictly defined by their social and cultural setting. In a fundamental sense, incorporation into Christ implied a new creation that manifested itself in the present (Gal 6:15; see also Gal 3:27-28). This conviction on the part of Paul underlies his insistence that in the age to come the very physical bodies of believers will undergo a transformation similar to Christ's own (1 Cor 15:50-57). In light of this glorious destiny awaiting the faithful, Paul believed that incorporation into Christ necessarily required an appropriate transformation of behavior in the sphere of one's ethical life. Both points can be seen in the following passage from Paul's Letter to the Romans: "Do you not know that all of us who have been baptized into Christ Jesus were baptized into his death? Therefore we have been buried with him by baptism into death, so that, just as Christ was raised from the dead by the glory of the Father, so we too might walk in newness of life" (Rom 6:3-4). In a manner reminiscent of Jesus' call to action found in the Sermon on the Mount (Matt 7:13-14), Paul employs in this passage the metaphor of walking in order to invite the Roman Christians to pursue ethically transformed lives in the present, which will anticipate imperfectly the *perfect* transformation at the close of the age. Although Paul firmly believes, then, that final salvation belongs to the future (see 1 Cor 15:24-28), he also taught that salvation could be actualized even now as a result of the renewal of one's ethical behavior toward God and one's neighbor (Gal 5:13-14).

   If we return now to the passage from 1 Corinthians 3:1-3, we see Paul emphasizing the necessity for those who confess Jesus as the crucified and resurrected Messiah to cultivate a value system that goes against the prevailing system in the surrounding Greco-Roman culture. We might say, in other words, that Paul urges the Corinthians to pursue a countercultural conduct of life. In keeping with this pastoral objective, Paul juxtaposes in 1 Corinthians 3:1-3 two types of persons: those who are spiritual and those who are fleshly. Paul is somewhat more forthcoming about what it means to rank among the latter. The fleshly appear as individuals who comport themselves in a decidedly *status quo* fashion. Indeed, if we translate the Greek of the passage as literally as possible, Paul's meaning is that the fleshly "walk" (*peripateite*; 1 Cor 3:3) along a path guided by ordinary human presuppositions concerning what counts as honorable. A logical inference is that those ranked among the spiritual walk along a different path. Paul cannot mean, however, that the latter behave in a nonhuman fashion, since Paul is concerned in both instances with human beings as moral subjects. What, then, does Paul mean?

Recognition of some of the fundamental anthropological and theological assumptions that guide the thinking of Paul sheds potential light on this question. Although Paul understands the human person as constituting what we might today call a psychosomatic unity, he also believes that human personhood encompasses distinct—though not separate—dimensions of the human personality.[8] The benediction that occurs at the conclusion of 1 Thessalonians provides a particularly helpful glimpse of the broad outlines of Paul's anthropology: "May the God of peace himself sanctify you entirely; and may your spirit and soul and body be kept sound and blameless at the coming of our Lord Jesus Christ" (1 Thess 5:23). Here Paul calls upon God to sanctify not isolated, component parts of a person, but instead the human person conceived as a totality. Put another way, each of the terms employed above by Paul represents a dimension of the human self or personality. Moreover, the use of the term "spirit" (*pneuma*) in 1 Thessalonians 5:23 signifies for Paul that dimension of the human self that is most open and responsive to transcendent reality,[9] in particular the transcendent reality made visible in the cruciform pattern of life embodied by Jesus. Here I employ the term cruciform as a way of referencing in a shorthand manner the total commitment of Jesus during his earthly ministry to live a life of self-sacrificial love on behalf of others, even to the point of dying

---

[8] For a discussion of these issues that remains helpful to this day see Rudolph Bultmann, *Theology of the New Testament*, vol 1, trans. Kendrick Grobel (New York: Charles Scribner's Sons, 1951), 209.

[9] For a detailed treatment of Paul's anthropological categories see James D. G. Dunn, *The Theology of Paul the Apostle* (Grand Rapids, MI: Eerdmans, 1998), 51–78. See also Bultmann, *Theology*, 191–210.

on the cross.[10] Such a commitment is especially visible in the gospel passion narratives, but it is also evident in the writings of Paul. For example, near the conclusion of an extended exhortation found in Galatians 5:13-6:5 that centers on the need for altruistic behavior in the community, Paul equates such behavior with the suggestion that selfless action on behalf of others fulfills the "law of Christ" (Gal 6:2). For Paul, the implication of this provocative phrase is clearly that the human Jesus embodied in his ministry a life of service for others that should serve as a model for the collective behavior of the faithful who now presently live in him.

For Paul, the opposite of spirit is not the body but instead the flesh, with flesh designating a particular attitude or sensibility that views life as having little connection to a deeper transcendent ground. As Paul understands the issue of community discord within the Corinthian community, expressions of envy and jealousy reveal just how deeply the Corinthians have bought into the competitive values of the surrounding culture (1 Cor 3:18-23; 11:20-22) and how little they have patterned their lives on the law of Christ (Gal 6:2), which for Paul means nothing other than a self-sacrificial or cruciform conduct of life lived for the benefit of others (see esp. Phil 2:3-6).

In addition to viewing the spirit as the most inward part of a person, Paul can also speak of the Spirit as a sphere of power that impacts an individual from outside oneself (Rom 8:1-2, 14; Gal 4:6). If we shift now from an anthropological to a more specifically theological perspective, what Paul seems to mean most fundamentally by the term "spiritual" is nothing other than a lived, personal encounter with God through the Spirit:[11]

> Now we have received not the spirit of the world, but the Spirit
> that is from God, so that we may understand the gifts bestowed
> on us by God. And we speak of these things in words not taught
> by human wisdom but taught by the Spirit [*pneumatos*], inter-

---

[10] See Michael J. Gorman, *Apostle of the Crucified Lord: A Theological Introduction to Paul and His Letters* (Grand Rapids, MI: Eerdmans, 2004), 140.

[11] See Walter Principe, "Toward Defining Spirituality," *SR* 12, no. 2 (1983), 127–41. See also Gorman, *Apostle*, 115.

preting spiritual things [*pneumatika*] to those who are spiritual [*pneumatikois*]. (1 Cor 2:12-13)

As Paul makes clear elsewhere in his letters (see Gal 4:6), the encounter with God through the Spirit is a deeply personal encounter. By virtue of the response of faith, believers receive the Spirit of God, the Spirit that is simultaneously that of the Spirit of Jesus, the Son of God. As a result of this encounter, the faithful are empowered to live out in concrete behavior the pattern of cruciform service for others that was exemplified in the life and death of Jesus (Rom 8:9-18; Gal 2:20). This is why Paul can boldly encourage the Galatian converts in Galatians 5 to "live," or better, to "walk" (*peripateite*) by the Spirit:

Live by the Spirit I say, and do not gratify the desires of the flesh. For what the flesh desires is opposed to the Spirit, and what the Spirit desires is opposed to the flesh; for these are opposed to each other, to prevent you from doing what you want. . . . the fruit of the Spirit is love, joy, peace, patience, kindness, generosity, faithfulness, gentleness, and self-control. (Gal 5:16-17, 22-23)

In this particular passage Paul invites his Galatian converts to pursue a countercultural existence in light of the transcendent and transformative power of the Spirit. Such an integration of the Spirit into daily life is anything but automatic. Indeed, Paul realistically sees that such integration entails struggle (Gal 5:17). Nevertheless, Paul understands conformity to the cruciform pattern of life exemplified in the life and death of Jesus as the essential goal of Christian existence this side of the age to come: "Do nothing from selfish ambition or conceit, but in humility regard others as better than yourselves. Let each of you look not to your own interests, but to the interests of others. Let the same mind be in you that was in Christ Jesus" (Phil 2:3-5). This passage calls to mind another passage, this one from the Gospel of Mark, where Jesus identifies himself as the Son of Man who "came not to be served but to serve, and to give his life a ransom for many" (Mark 10:45).

I find myself persuaded that Paul gives expression in a more existentially immediate fashion to a religious experience, which various scholars of spirituality convey with far more abstract terminology. Michael Downey, for example, writes that, "spirituality broadly understood refers to the quest for personal integration in light of levels of reality not immediately apparent."[12] The noted Roman Catholic biblical scholar Sandra M. Schneiders offers a similar, if somewhat more technical, definition: "spirituality refers to the experience of consciously striving to integrate one's life in terms not of isolation and self-absorption but of self-transcendence toward the ultimate value one perceives."[13] Both of these definitions of spirituality privilege what I would describe as the idea of the luminescence of the transcendent within concrete human experience. With the important caveat in place that Paul never actually employs the term *spirituality*, my own guess is that Paul would have found these two definitions of the spiritual life congenial to his way of thinking about the essential nature of Christian discipleship. Since Paul was not a systematic theologian, however, the language he uses for giving expression to his particular vision of the spiritual life is decidedly more participatory in character. In place of such phrases as self-transcendence and personal integration, Paul speaks more characteristically of union with Christ: "I have been crucified with Christ; and it is no longer I who live, but it is Christ who lives in me" (Gal 2:19-20). Another passage illustrative of this theme of concrete participation in Christ is Philippians 3:10-11: "I want to know Christ and the power of his resurrection and the sharing of his suffering by becoming like him in his death, if somehow I may attain the resurrection from the dead."

In the pages to follow, I propose that this understanding of spirituality as illustrative of the idea of the luminescence of the transcendent within concrete human experience also animates the

---

[12] Downey, *Understanding*, 32.

[13] Sandra M. Schneiders, "The Study of Christian Spirituality: Contours and Dynamics of a Discipline," in *Minding the Spirit: The Study of Christian Spirituality*, ed. Elisabeth A. Dreyer and Mark S. Burrows (Baltimore: Johns Hopkins, 2004), 5–6.

early Christian text known as the Letter to the Hebrews, a text sometimes associated with Paul, but almost certainly written by someone other than the apostle to the Gentiles. I suspect that not a few readers who are familiar with the contents of this particular New Testament writing may respond to this claim with a certain measure of incredulity. Over several years of teaching this letter, I have encountered a significant number of students who have felt that Hebrews assigns too overwhelming a prominence to the eternal and heavenly at the expense of the transitory and visible (see 7:15; 8:4-5; 9:11-14; 12:27). Indeed, a question I frequently hear from my students concerns whether such a text can truly serve as a resource for personal growth and integration in the context of daily living with all of its visible and concrete concerns? Although I understand this apprehension, I think that the emphasis one finds in Hebrews on the surpassing value of the transcendent dimension is no less a feature of the writings attributed to Paul, who also looks to the future consummation of all things as the destiny for those incorporated in Christ (see Phil 3:20; 1 Cor 15:50-57). One can, I think, make the same claim for the historical Jesus. For while the Synoptic Gospels remember Jesus as a prophetic figure who challenged the economic and social exploitation of the poor by the powerful elites of his day (see Mark 11:17; 12:38-40), these same sources also remember him as an apocalyptic prophet who envisioned the dramatic end of days (see Mark 13:24-27). Indeed it seems likely that Jesus' apocalyptic vision significantly influenced his program of covenant renewal.

A glance at the Lord's Prayer more than confirms this impression. There the petition to God both to provide bread (Luke 11:3; Matt 6:11) and remit debts (Matt 6:12) assuredly affords a glimpse into the impoverished peasant population that was the target audience for Jesus' historical ministry (Luke 6:20-21). At the same time, the Lord's Prayer also petitions God to establish God's kingdom on earth (Luke 11:2; Matt 6:10); this is a petition that envisions the end of the age or at the very least a transformed cosmos in the age to come.[14] My point here is simply that the perceived

---

[14] See Bultmann, *Theology*, 4.

otherworldliness of Hebrews may actually be consistent with the largely apocalyptic character of both the ministry of Jesus and much of the earliest literature that emanated from the primitive Christian movement.

While I think it is important to acknowledge the apocalyptic character of Hebrews, at the same time I consider it is a mistake to think of this letter as being in some way unconcerned with the integration of the transcendent dimension within concrete human experience. There are simply too many instances in the letter where we see the author take significant pains to encourage specific behaviors in light of theological commitments to maintain such a position (see 2:1-3; 4:14-16; 10:36; 13:1-6). Moreover, while one cannot deny the impression conveyed by Hebrews that heavenly realities are superior to earthly realities (3:1; 6:4; 9:23), this does not mean that the earthly and heavenly are thoroughly opposed to each other. In fact, any thoroughgoing opposition between these two realities is precluded, since the person of Jesus functions in Hebrews as the human model for how the path of integration should ideally take place. This is borne out not least of all by the deeply participatory emphasis of Hebrews' incarnational theology: "Since, therefore, the children share flesh and blood, he himself likewise shared the same things" (2:14). Somewhat later in the same chapter the author also observes that Jesus "had to become like his brothers and sisters in every respect" (2:17). And perhaps most importantly of all, Jesus is described in Hebrews as a high priest who was tested in every way that human beings are (4:15). Like Paul, then, the author of Hebrews also displays a lively interest in the paradigmatic significance of Jesus' life and death.

This last observation is particularly crucial to accentuate. Throughout this study I will aim to demonstrate that one of the major christological themes that one consistently meets in Hebrews is the theme of Jesus as the perfect high priest, who, on account of his own human response of fidelity before God, has made it possible for others to attain to communion with God (7:19, 25). This emphasis on the response of Jesus' fidelity or faithfulness before God will serve as the principal christological prism through which the spirituality of the Letter to the Hebrews will shine forth.

   This book will unfold in four chapters. Chapter 1 is an attempt
to situate Hebrews within its historical, literary, and social context.
In addition to addressing foundational issues associated with such
questions as the authorship, social location, and ethnic makeup
of Hebrews, I endeavor to sketch in this chapter (1) the broad
contours of the challenging social situation that the audience of
Hebrews faced and (2) how the author responds to this situation
in a pastorally meaningful manner. Although the title of theologian is more applicable to the author of Hebrews than it is to Paul,
like Paul the author is equally concerned with the task of framing
his often-complex theological reflection as a response to concrete
experiences within the community. In chapter 2, I analyze the
distinctive christological vision of Jesus as an eternal high priest.
Central to this chapter will be a discussion of the importance that
the theme of the perfection of Jesus has for appreciating the vision
of spirituality presented in Hebrews. I propose in the second chapter that a key feature of the Christocentric spirituality of Hebrews
is to be found in its portrayal of Jesus as the representative Son of
God who lived a life of supreme fidelity or faithfulness before God.
Noting the strong journey motif contained in Hebrews, I analyze
in chapter 3 the shape of the nature of salvation, which the author
of Hebrews envisions as both a future and a present reality for the
faithful. I demonstrate that while the author understands salvation
to refer ultimately to a future reality, even now the community is
invited to live out their salvation on the basis of their existential
awareness of a cleansed conscience. Lastly, given the author's use
of the Jewish Bible to shape and form the identity of his audience,
I provide an exegetical analysis in chapter 4 that focuses on how
the specific scriptural figure of Abel functions in Hebrews as a
lens through which to view the deeper significance of the sacrificial activity of Jesus, a distinctive feature of the Christology of this
letter.

Chapter 1

Hebrews in Historical Context

We begin our exploration of the spirituality of Hebrews by charting the contours of the historical, literary, and social context behind the letter. In a study devoted to the topic of the spirituality of Hebrews, I am aware that the reader may be surprised to see relatively detailed observations on such apparent background issues as the authorship, intended audience, and purpose of the letter. The very persons who would readily agree that matters such as these are appropriate issues for investigation in a biblical commentary might wonder at the proposed relevance of these same issues for appreciating the vision of the spiritual life articulated in Hebrews. This question is a fair one and so deserves an explanation on my part from the outset. Although I am convinced that Hebrews has much to offer in terms of contemporary relevance, it is important to remember that Hebrews was not written for us, at least not primarily so. A clear sighted recognition of the very different cultural and historical setting in which the writings of the New Testament emerged can go a long way in helping us to discern something of the original meaning that the ancient authors of these texts primarily intended. The historical work that will engage our attention in this chapter, therefore, will contextualize and thereby intellectually inform and enrich the valid project of the contemporary application of Hebrews. Cunningham and Egan put the matter in these terms: "As we query texts from the past it is crucial to be sensitive to the cultural situation of these texts. Such sensitivity permits us to read in a manner that allows us to disentangle what is peculiar to a given time but not useful for our own and, equally frees us from the temptation to a kind of spiritual fundamentalism."[1] In addition to this concern for what we might call the world behind the text, my rationale for reflecting on such issues as the intended audience and purpose of Hebrews stems from the definition of spirituality that I have proposed above. If, as I have maintained, Christian spirituality has to do with the lived experience of an encounter with the transcendent presence of God as reveled in the life, death, and resurrection of Jesus, then it makes sense to explore from a historical perspective the principal evidence, supplying what Sandra Schneiders has called the "positive data of the Christian religious experience"— namely, Scripture.[2]

Throughout the anthology of writings that is the canonical New Testament, we encounter the diverse voices of ancient Christians striving to put into words their conviction that God was present and active in Jesus. What we find in the pages of Scripture, therefore, is neither a collection of abstract theological propositions nor a neutral historical account, but instead a rich testimony to a personal encounter with the divine. We might say that ultimately what we see in the books of the New Testament is the imprint of powerful spiritual experiences; and what we hear are the echoes of personal testimonies to lived revelatory encounters with God. It is important to remember, however, that Scripture does not give expression to what we might call a universal or a-contextual spirituality. Every experience or encounter with transcendent or ultimate power is inevitably shaped by the social and historical setting in which that encounter takes place. And it is only by paying close attention to such social and historical particularity that substantive glimpses into the essence of that encounter become available for analysis.

Nevertheless, the totality of the experiential encounter that lies at the heart of every spiritual experience is largely unrecoverable. For example, although we discern something of the outline of Paul's deeply personal experience of encountering the risen Jesus

---

[1] Cunnningham and Egan, *Christian Spirituality*, 17. See also Thomas H. Tobin, *The Spirituality of Paul* (Eugene: Wipf and Stock, 2008), 12.

[2] Schneiders, "The Study of Christian Spirituality," 7.

when we observe Paul's own description of this event (see Gal 1:15-16), we can never enter completely into the full dimensions of that encounter as it was experienced by Paul. Indeed, Paul himself is quite reticient in his letters about the precise nature of his encounter with the risen Jesus. Both Galatians 1:15 and 1 Corinthians 15:8 suggest that Paul saw something in his encounter with the risen Jesus, but these passages remain nonetheless quite cryptic. Even the more familiar yet strongly legendary accounts of Paul's encounter with the risen Jesus that are described in the book of Acts (9:3-8; 22:4-16; 26:9-18) are more suggestive than they are descriptive.

The author of Hebrews similarly speaks of powerful yet allusive religious experiences that both he and his listeners have shared in the past. Such experiences apparently included the working of miracles (2:4), intellectual enlightenment (6:4), the confidence of a cleansed conscience (9:14; 10:2), as well as an overwhelming communal perception of sharing in the power of God's Spirit (2:4; 6:4). Powerful experiences of religious immediacy such as these demand interpretation at the level of intellectual appropriation if they are to endure beyond the moment. This suggests that the liberation theologian Gustavo Gutiérrez is correct when he describes the second stage within the development of a spiritual tradition as that stage where "spiritual experience becomes a subject for reflection."[3] Much like Paul does in his letters, so, too, in Hebrews, the author offers to the community the fruit of his own substantial theological reflection. Indeed, the importance of this intellectual task is signaled by the author's challenge to his audience near the conclusion of chapter 5: "About this we have much to say that is hard to explain, since you have become dull in understanding. For though by this time you ought to be teachers, you need someone to teach you again the basic elements of the oracles of God" (5:11-12). It would be a mistake, however, were we to regard Hebrews simply as an exercise in abstract systematic theology. In company with Paul, but with significantly sharper theological instincts, the author of Hebrews exhibits considerable

---

[3] Gustavo Gutiérrez, *We Drink from Our Own Wells: The Spiritual Journey of a People*, 20th anniversary ed., trans. Matthew J. O'Connell (Maryknoll: Orbis, 2003), 52.

personal investment in the lives of the ancient Christians who were the original recipients of the letter. Writing with a pastoral knowledge of where this audience finds itself at the present moment in history, our author endeavors to transform the collective experience, as well as the ethical behavior, of his audience through a creative explication of the deeper significance of the Christ event.

Authorship

As is the case with numerous other writings contained in the New Testament, the precise authorship of Hebrews is impossible to determine with certainty. Most modern translations of the New Testament place Hebrews at the end of the Pauline correspondence preceded by the letters addressed to churches and to individuals. This arrangement suggests a tendency both to associate Paul with Hebrews and to distance the apostle to the Gentiles from this first century homily.[4] Since some of the earliest Greek manuscripts of Hebrews include the letter among the letters of Paul, it is probable that by the early third century many considered Paul to have been the author of Hebrews. Various early church writers echo this assessment, while at the same time recognizing that Hebrews is dissimilar in important respects to the letters attributed to Paul.

The earliest references to the topic of the authorship of Hebrews derive from Christian circles active in the eastern half of the Roman Empire.[5] According to a testimony preserved in the fourth century *Ecclesiastical History* of Eusebius, Clement of Alexandria in the second century believed that Paul composed Hebrews *in* Hebrew for a Jewish audience. Noting similarities in style between the book of Acts and Hebrews, Clement believed that it was Paul's traveling companion Luke (Col 4:14; Phlm 24) who translated

---

[4] The designation of Hebrews as a sermon in letter form is increasingly emphasized in contemporary scholarship on the letter. See Judith Hoch Wray, *Rest as a Theological Metaphor in the Epistle to the Hebrews and the Gospel of Truth: Early Christian Homilectics of Rest*, SBLDS 166 (Atlanta: Scholars Press, 1998), 52.

[5] See the detailed discussion of the varied historical issues pertaining to the study of Hebrews in the recent commentary of Craig R. Koester; see Craig R. Koester, *Hebrews: A New Translation with Introduction and Commentary*, AB 36 (New York: Doubleday, 2001), 19–79.

Hebrews into Greek for a more universal audience (Eusebius, *Hist. eccl.* 6.14.2). A somewhat different appraisal of Pauline authorship appears in the comments of the great scriptural theologian and student of Clement, Origen. Observing the rhetorical sophistication and elevated Greek style of Hebrews, Origen supposed that Paul dictated the letter in Greek but that some unknown individual did the actual work of composition (Eusebius, *Hist. eccl.* 6. 25.13). By the time Eusebius was writing in the fourth century, some of the more popular candidates for Origen's anonymous author included Luke—the traditional author of the third Gospel and the book of Acts—as well as Clement of Rome (Eusebius, *Hist. eccl.* 3.38.2; 6.25.14) and Barnabas (Tertullian, *De pudicitia* 20). The scholarly reservations of Origen notwithstanding, Christians in the eastern part of the empire widely regarded Hebrews as an authoritative writing of Paul. This situation went unduplicated, however, in the western part of the empire, where it was not until the fifth century that the reception of Hebrews as a Pauline letter became secure.[6]

Few scholars today would want to defend the position that Paul wrote Hebrews. This reluctance stems from the recognition of certain stylistic as well as thematic differences that appear when one compares Hebrews with the uncontested letters of Paul.[7] For example, although Hebrews concludes in a manner reminiscent of Paul's letters with the mention of a personal name (Timothy)

---

[6] Augustine notes the following: "Many important things are written about Melchizedek in the epistle entitled To the Hebrews, which the majority attribute to apostle Paul, though some deny the attribution" (City of God 16.22). St. Augustine, *Concerning the City of God against the Pagans, A New Tranlsation by Henry Bettenson with an Introduction by John O'Meara* (Penguin Classics, 1984), 680.

[7] There exists a wide consensus among contemporary scholars that the following letters were certainly written by Paul: Romans, 1 and 2 Corinthians, Galatians, 1 Thessalonians, Philippians, and Philemon. Opinions vary as to whether the six other letters attributed to Paul in the NT canon should be thought of as pseudonymous or written in the name of Paul: 2 Thessalonians, Colossians, Ephesians, 1 and 2 Timothy, and Titus. If, however, one considers authorship in a manner that leaves room for indirect agency, it is possible that Paul may have had varying degrees of connection to each of the letters attributed to him in the canon. For this argument, see Luke Timothy Johnson, *Among the Gentiles: Greco-Roman Religion and Christianity* (New Haven: Yale University Press, 2009), x.

as well a brief travel notice (see 13:23), the letter lacks the kind of formal introduction that is a consistent feature of Paul's correspondence (see Rom 1:1-7; 1 Cor 1:1-3; 2 Cor 1:1-2; 1 Thess 1:1-3; Gal 1:1-2; Phil 1:1-2; Phlm 1–3). In place of a brief notice signifying the sender and addressee, Hebrews commences instead with a lengthy christological reflection that focuses on the heavenly exaltation of the Son (1:1-14). Further stylistic differences between Hebrews and Paul are evident as well. For example, whereas Paul tends to allocate sections of communal exhortation either near the middle (see Rom 14:1–15:13) or conclusion of his letters (see Gal 5:13–6:10), Hebrews prefers a pattern where exhortation and theological exposition alternate throughout the letter.[8] In company with Paul, the author of Hebrews frequently pursues theological reflection in conversation with the Jewish Bible. Indeed the author's familiarity with a wide range of discrete scriptural texts and foundational stories is frequently on display in the letter, particularly in chapter 11 where one encounters an elaborate speech of praise in honor of the faithful responses of numerous figures from both the Jewish Bible as well as certain deuterocanonical texts. However, in contrast to Paul, who typically introduces quotes from Scripture with the phrase: "as it has been written" (Rom 3:10; 8:36; 9:13), the author of Hebrews cites Scripture in a far more complex manner as either the direct speech of the Holy Spirit, an anonymous speaker, or even God (3:7, 15; 5:5-6; 10:15; 12:5; 4:3; 2:6). Hebrews also diverges from Paul in terms of some of its most distinctive theological emphases. Most notably, while on occasion Paul can assess the significance of the Christ event with the help of sacrificial categories (see Rom 3:25; Gal 1:4), there is little in Paul's letters that matches the elaborate understanding of atonement encountered in Hebrews, where Jesus appears as an eternal high priest whose death atones completely for sin and cleanses the conscience of the believer (9:9, 14, 22, 26; 10:2, 22).

We have already noted Origen's suspicion that someone other than Paul wrote Hebrews. In both the ancient and modern periods

---

[8] See Harold W. Attridge, *The Epistle to the Hebrews: A Commentary on the Epistle to the Hebrews*, Hermeneia (Philadelphia: Fortress, 1989), 63.

we find suggestions that one of Paul's missionary associates may have composed the letter. Near the conclusion of it, the author suggestively mentions the figure of Timothy (13:23), who in all probability refers to the same Timothy whom Paul characterizes as a beloved fellow messenger of the Gospel (Phil 2:20-22). Given the fact that Hebrews concludes like a typical Pauline letter with a formal postscript (13:20-25), it is possible that someone added the name Timothy at some point in the textual transmission of Hebrews in an attempt to associate the letter more closely with Paul.[9] Even if Timothy is not the author of Hebrews—which he likely is not—the appearance of his personal name in 13:23 could suggest that someone in the Pauline mission field was responsible for the production of Hebrews. Besides Timothy, the figures most frequently mentioned as potential candidates for authorship include Prisca, Barnabas, and Apollos.[10] Of these, the figure of Apollos is especially intriguing, since he appears elsewhere in the New Testament as a polished speaker, as well as a gifted interpreter of Scripture—qualities that are fitting appellations for describing the author of Hebrews (see Acts 18:24; 1 Cor 1:12-3:21).[11] That said, there were undoubtedly other early Christian missionaries who possessed similar rhetorical abilities. While speculation concerning the identity of the author of Hebrews can be an intriguing intellectual exercise, it is probably best to agree with the assessment of Alan Mitchell who, guided by Origen's reflections on the issue of Hebrews' authorship, suggests that Hebrews should be viewed as an anonymous document.[12]

Literary Observations

More consequential than speculation on the authorship of Hebrews is an appreciation for the text that we have before us. On this issue, one should not let the complexity of the theological

[9] See Clare K. Rothschild, *Hebrews as Pseudepigraphan: The History and Significance of the Pauline Attribution of Hebrews*, WUNT 235 (Tübingen: Mohr Siebeck, 2009).

[10] See Luke Timothy Johnson, *Hebrews: A Commentary*, New Testament Library (Louisville: Westminster John Knox Press, 2003), 40–44.

[11] See Johnson, *Hebrews*, 43.

[12] Alan C. Mitchell, *Hebrews*, SP 13 (Collegeville, MN: Liturgical Press, 2007), 6.

reflection of Hebrews deflect one from appreciating the sophisti-
cated literary artistry of this sermon. Like the vast majority of the
texts contained in the New Testament, Hebrews was written to be
heard (13:22), and the anonymous author has carefully crafted the
letter to exert a persuasive, as well as a pleasing, effect upon the
listener.[13] Whatever tentative conclusions one might draw pertaining to the possible identity of the author of Hebrews, it is all but
certain that he was well acquainted with the art of persuasion, or
more commonly, *rhetoric*.[14] Even a basic acquaintance with some
of the rhetorical tools of antiquity can help us better appreciate
the essentially pastoral purpose of Hebrews.

Generally speaking, ancient theorists of the art of rhetoric beginning with Aristotle conceived of three forms or genres of public
speaking: forensic, deliberative, demonstrative, or epideictic. Each
of these genres was, in turn, characterized by a pronounced temporal emphasis. Forensic speeches were principally concerned
with persuading an audience about the truth of some matter that
had taken place in the past. A good example from the New Testament of a text that reveals forensic qualities is Paul's Letter to the
Galatians. Much of this letter is devoted to Paul's passionate de-
fense of the adequacy of the response of faith for Gentile converts
to become justified or rightly related to God. For Paul, it was the
response of faith, not the observance of Torah legislation, that
bestowed the gift of the Spirit upon Gentile converts in the past
(see Gal 3:1-2). The second major genre of oratory was called deliberative. Concerned with the task of encouraging an audience
to adopt certain behaviors or a future course of action, deliberative
speeches were necessarily future oriented. An example of delib-

---

[13] In a recent study, David deSilva offers a most helpful and accessible description
of the rhetorical proficiency of Hebrews. See David deSilva, *The Letter to the Hebrews
in Social Science Perspective* (Eugene: Cascade, 2012), 3–9. The author of Hebrews
demonstrates particular skill in the use of alliteration, which is most clearly evident
in the original Greek of the letter. For example, five of the twelve words that comprise
the opening verse of Hebrews begin with the Greek letter Pi: *polumerōs, polutropōs,
palai, patrasin, prophētais.*

[14] Although Hebrews should be viewed as anonymous, the occurrence in Greek of
a masculine participle in 11:32 confirms that the unknown author was male.

erative rhetoric appears in Paul's discussion of weak and strong Christians found in Romans 14 and 15. Paul's rhetorical goal in these chapters is to convince both groups of Christians to live in harmony with one another (see Rom 15:7-9).[15] The third genre of oratory was called demonstrative or epideictic. These speeches focused on the present and invited the members of an audience to celebrate shared commitments that they already cherished.[16] The birth accounts of Jesus found in the early chapters of Matthew and Luke (Matt 1:18–2:23 & Luke 1:5–2:52) offer especially good examples of this genre. Although the presence of legendary elements in the New Testament accounts of the birth of Jesus does not automatically exclude the possibility that these narratives preserve traditions having some basis in historical fact, it is important to emphasize that objective historical reporting is far from the intention of the gospel authors, who are principally concerned with theological proclamation.[17] The creative mix of legend and midrash on the Jewish Bible found in the Synoptic birth narratives functions largely to praise the honor of Jesus and to confirm for the faithful who first heard these accounts that God was present in Jesus from the very moment of his conception. In this sense, the infancy narratives function as epideictic speeches of praise.

Since much of Hebrews is devoted to a celebration of the heavenly and eternal priesthood of Christ that enables renewed access to God, the genre of demonstrative or epideictic oratory seems the best match for the letter overall. Nevertheless, since significant sections of the letter also call upon the audience to contemplate anew their understanding of Jesus' identity (6:1) and to emulate the radical faithfulness of Jesus (12:2), elements of deliberative oratory are in evidence as well. On balance, we might say that the

---

[15] See Kevin B. McCruden, "Judgment and Life for the Lord: Occasion and Theology of Romans 14, 1–15, 13," *Bib* 86 (2005), 229–44.

[16] See David E. Aune, *The New Testament in Its Literary Environment*, Library of Early Christianity (Philadelphia: Fortress Press, 1987), 198–99.

[17] Raymond Brown considers a noticeably early birth of Jesus to be potentially one of these historical memories. See Raymond E. Brown, *The Birth of the Messiah: A Commentary on the Infancy Narratives in Matthew and Luke* (New York: Doubleday, 1977), 527.

essentially demonstrative or epideictic christology of Hebrews serves the deliberative goal of strengthening the religious commitment of an audience so that it might persevere in its faith commitment: "Do not, therefore, abandon that confidence of yours; it brings a great reward. For you need endurance, so that when you have done the will of God, you may receive what was promised" (10:35-36).

The Intended Audience of Hebrews

Since the author nowhere identifies the intended recipients of his sermon, it is difficult to determine the makeup of the original audience for Hebrews. The letter was obviously written for persons who professed a faith commitment in Jesus as God's agent of salvation (see 1:14; 2:3, 10; 5:9; 6:9). It also seems likely that second generation believers evangelized by earlier Christian missionaries comprised the majority of the original audience (see 2:3; 13:7).[18] But does the letter provide any additional clues that might help us discern the ethnic makeup of its intended audience? Employing categories that are to some extent anachronistic for the period under investigation, were the first recipients of Hebrews Jewish Christians, Gentile Christians, or a mixture of both? And perhaps more importantly, would knowledge of the ethnic and religious status of the audience contribute in any meaningful way to an informed interpretation of the letter?

We saw above that Clement of Alexandria envisioned Luke translating a letter that was originally sent by Paul to a Jewish Christian audience. The earliest Greek papyrus that contains Hebrews (P 46) lists the title of the letter as *Pros Ebraious* or "To the Hebrews." Might both these factors suggest that Hebrews targeted an audience comprised of Jewish Christians? Some scholars have thought as much. Prominent among contemporary advocates for the position that Hebrews was written for a Jewish-Christian audi-

---

[18] According to deSilva, the author's reference to "those who heard him" (2:3)—namely, Jesus (2:3)—strongly suggests that Paul cannot have been the author of Hebrews, since Paul attributes his faith in Jesus to a direct encounter with the risen Lord. See deSilva, *The Letter*, 2.

ence is Barnabas Lindars, who maintains that Hebrews addresses a community comprised of Jewish Christians who have come to doubt the adequacy of the death of Jesus to atone completely for sin.[19] Lindars maintains that in response to this particular crisis the author sketches a portrait of Christ as an eternal high priest who provides a forever abiding heavenly intercession for the faithful. An integral component of this proposal is the assumption that the Jewish audience targeted by Hebrews felt the pull of the familiar patterns of Jewish liturgical practices that had formerly shaped their religious identity.[20] Perceiving the potential for the community to relapse, the author responds by emphasizing the adequacy of the atonement achieved by Christ's sacrificial death.

The strength of this proposal is twofold. First, it displays sensitivity to the highly sacrificial tone of Hebrews by taking seriously the letter's focus on the atonement secured by the death and exaltation of Jesus (10:12-14). Second, this proposal also provides a coherent explanation for the frequent passages of warning scattered throughout the letter that depict the danger of communal apostasy (see esp. 2:1-3; 3:12; 4:1-3). For Lindars, these warnings testify to the author's perception that the audience was in danger of reverting back to their former Jewish customs and beliefs.

Despite these strengths, several problems accompany this particular reconstruction of the purpose of Hebrews. First, nowhere in the letter do we encounter unambiguous evidence that the community addressed by Hebrews was either anxious about atonement or was contemplating a return to the security of more familiar Jewish liturgical patterns. On the contrary, when the author refers to the atonement secured by the heavenly enthronement of Jesus, the prevailing tone appears to be one of celebration of a conviction already shared by the author and community alike (see 9:14; 10:10, 19-22).[21] Second, while it is accurate to maintain that

---

[19] Barnabas Lindars, *The Theology of the Letter to the Hebrews*, New Testament Theology (Cambridge: Cambridge University Press, 1991), 4–12.

[20] Ibid., 4.

[21] To be precise, I do not think that the author's specific portrait of Jesus as heavenly high priest was already familiar to the audience. The author appears to be the first to connect the traditional belief in the exaltation of Jesus known from many other

the author frequently addresses the dangers of faithlessness, the root cause of the potential for communal apostasy was more likely connected to feelings of disillusionment and discouragement rather than to a renewed attraction for former religious commitments. Indeed, apart from the title, "To the Hebrews,"—which was likely added sometime after its composition—there is little in the letter that necessitates the supposition of a strictly Jewish-Christian audience. Neither does the author's expectation that the audience would resonate with the narratives of the Jewish Bible demand a Jewish audience, since Paul assumes a similar knowledge on the part of his Gentile converts.[22] Indeed, the dangers associated with mirror reading the historical situation of Hebrews's audience based on the perceived "Jewishness" of the content of the letter is especially apparent in this reconstruction.

While in the past I was inclined to view the intended audience of Hebrews as a mixed community comprised of Jews and Gentiles, I now think that Hebrews supplies slightly more evidence for a community comprised primarily, if not exclusively, of Gentiles.[23] Two examples might help clarify this impression. First, as part of his summons to the audience to press on toward perfection or maturity (6:1), the author reprises what appear to be elements of the initial conversion experience of at least some of the members of the community: "Therefore let us go on toward perfection, leaving behind the basic teaching about Christ, and not laying again the foundation: repentance from dead works and faith

---

Christian texts to the notice in Psalm 110:4 concerning the priesthood of Melchizedek. This particular christological twist owes much to the author's creative reading of Jewish Scripture.

[22] This is evident from 1 Corinthians 10:1-5, where Paul assumes that his Gentile readers are familiar with the scriptural traditions associated with the Exodus. Interestingly, the author of Hebrews apparently assumes the same about his audience (see 3:7-19).

[23] Other scholars have noted the possibility of at least a substantial Gentile presence included among Hebrews's audience. See Patrick Gray, "Hebrews Among Greeks and Romans," in *Reading the Epistle to the Hebrews: A Resource for Students*, ed. Eric F. Mason and Kevin B. McCruden, SBLRBS 66 (Atlanta: Society of Biblical Literature, 2011), 14; Alan C. Mitchell, "A Sacrifice of Praise: Does Hebrews Promote Supersessionism?" in *Reading the Epistle*, 254–55; deSilva, *The Letter*, 35.

toward God, instruction about baptisms, laying on of hands, resurrection of the dead, and eternal judgment" (6:1-2). In this passage, the author characterizes the community's collective response of "repentance from dead works and faith toward God" as constituting what he calls the "basic teaching about Christ" (6:1). The author includes among this "basic teaching" such practices as ceremonial washings, the laying on of hands, as well more existential matters relating to the assurance of the resurrection of the dead and eternal judgment (6:2). One is reminded in all this of the similar exhortation that Paul directs to his exclusively Gentile audience in 1 Thessalonians, where he describes the conversion experience of the Thessalonian converts as a turning aside from idols in order to "serve a living and true God" (1 Thess 1:9). In that letter, Paul proceeds to assure the community that, as a consequence of repudiating their idolatrous past, they can now look forward to the return of the resurrected Jesus, who will deliver them from God's impending wrath (see 1 Thess 1:10). In keeping with his customary interest in moral identity formation, Paul encourages his Gentile converts toward the conclusion of 1 Thessalonians to embody countercultural lives marked by ethically pure behavior (1 Thess 4:1-8), especially in the area of sexuality: "For this is the will of God, your sanctification: that you abstain from fornication; that each one of you know how to control your own body in holiness and honor, not with lustful passion, like the Gentiles who do not know God. . . . For God did not call us to impurity but in holiness" (1 Thess 4:3-7). In other words, Paul calls upon the Thessalonians to renounce what one might characterize as "dead works" (Heb 6:1) in pursuit of the effort to give concrete expression to their new identity in God's Spirit (see 1 Thess 4:8). Here we once again see Paul's conviction that salvation has a present dimension which is expressed primarily through a morally transformed life.

In a similar manner, Hebrews links "repentance" in 6:1 with both a turning aside from immoral behavior ("dead works") and the expectation of resurrection and future judgment by God. Complementing Paul's insistence upon the necessity for holiness of life, the author likewise warns the community that God will judge sexually immoral persons (13:4; see also 1 Thess 4:6-8). And, like Paul, the author of Hebrews frequently designates God as "living" (3:12; 9:14; 10:31; 12:22). While there is a tendency among some scholars to refer to the mixed audiences behind Paul's letters, there is really little evidence to suggest that in 1 Thessalonians Paul was addressing anything less than an exclusively Gentile audience. The verbal and thematic parallels noted above provide suggestive clues that the audience targeted by Hebrews may also have been largely, if not exclusively, comprised of Gentiles as well.

Second, beginning in 5:11 a noticeable shift in tone ensues as the author censures the audience for their apparent intellectual immaturity:

> About this we have much to say that is hard to explain, since you have become dull in understanding. For though by this time you ought to be teachers, you need someone to teach you again the basic elements of the oracles of God. You need milk, not solid food; for everyone who lives on milk, being still an infant, is unskilled in the word of righteousness. But solid food is for the mature, for those whose faculties have been trained by practice to distinguish good from evil. (5:11-14).

In his analysis of this passage, Craig Koester helpfully notes that such sudden criticism of the audience functions as a rhetorical digression designed to jolt the audience to renewed attention in preparation for the extended reflection that the author will devote to the topic of the eternal priesthood of Christ beginning in chapter seven.[24] Koester argues that the persuasive power of this digression derives in large measure from the images of milk and solid food (5:12), images that were commonly employed in antiquity as both philosophical and educational metaphors.[25] By identifying the audience as immature children (5:13) incapable of grasping more complex reflection on the significance of Christ, the author

[24] Koester, *Hebrews*, 306–7.
[25] DeSilva, *The Letter*, 13–14.

seeks to rouse the personal indignation of the audience in the hopes of securing their renewed attention to the sermon.[26]

While Koester's reflections on the rhetorical significance of this passage are well taken, I wonder whether the passage may also offer potential clues into the ethnic and religious identity of the original auditors of Hebrews. Once again, Paul affords a useful comparison. In 1 Corinthians 3:1-4 Paul rebukes the socially privileged members of the Corinthian congregation for aligning themselves competitively with Christian missionaries such as Apollos, who apparently appeared more rhetorically gifted than Paul (see 1 Cor 2:1-5 and 2 Cor 10:10).[27] Characterizing those engaged in such posturing as "fleshly" persons (1 Cor 3:1), who behave in a merely "human" manner (1 Cor 3:3), Paul attempts to shame the individuals responsible for such divisive behavior by comparing them to children who are ready for milk and not solid food (1 Cor 3:1-2). In describing their respective audiences as immature children, it is likely that both Paul and the author of Hebrews are displaying a shared sensibility that viewed the larger Gentile world as in need of guidance. Such a sensibility was already given traditional expression in the Jewish Bible as evidenced by such texts as Isaiah 2:2-4: "In days to come the mountain of the LORD's house shall be established as the highest of the mountains, and shall be raised above the hills; all the nations shall stream to it. Many peoples shall come and say, 'Come, let us go up to the mountain of the LORD, to the house of the God of Jacob; that he may teach us his ways and that we may walk in his paths.'" The reference in this passage to the Lord giving instruction to the

---

[26] Koester, *Hebrews*, 308. A very helpful discussion of ancient Greek pedagogical theory in relation to this section of Hebrews can be found in James W. Thompson, *The Beginnings of Christian Philosophy: The Epistle to the Hebrews*, CBQMS 13 (Washington: Catholic Biblical Association, 1982), 17–40.

[27] Maria Pascuzzi argues that the elite members of the Corinthian community were denigrating Paul by labeling him as a mere baptizer as opposed to an eloquent preacher. According to Pascuzzi, such defamation of Paul accounts for Paul's attempt in 1 Cor 1:14-16 to distance himself from his own prior baptismal activity in Corinth. See Maria Pascuzzi, "Baptism-based Allegiance and the Divisions in Corinth: A Reexamination of 1 Corinthians 1:13-17," *CBQ* 71 (2009): 813–29.

nations so that they might know the Lord's will takes on added
resonance when read in light of Romans 2:17-20:

> But if you call yourself a Jew and rely on the law and boast of
> your relation to God and know his will and determine what is
> best because you are instructed in the law, and if you are sure
> that you are a guide to the blind, a light to those who are in
> darkness, a corrector of the foolish, a teacher of children, having
> in the law the embodiment of knowledge and truth, you, then,
> that teach others, will you not teach yourself? . . . You that
> boast in the law, do you dishonor God by breaking the law?
> For as it is written, "the name of God is blasphemed among the
> Gentiles because of you."

Much as a modern day stand-up comedian assumes the role of
different characters as part of his or her onstage routine, Paul
employs in this section of Romans the ancient rhetorical tool called
the diatribe in which he engages in a mock conversation with an
imaginary partner.[28] Two features stand out in Paul's mock conversation. First, Paul's conversation partner is a Jew. Second, Paul
agrees with the assessment that Gentiles are, by and large, foolish,
childish, and blind with respect to the knowledge of God. In other
words, Paul agrees with his interlocutor that faithful Jews, by
virtue of their covenant status with God, are in a position to correct and guide Gentiles when it comes to discerning God's will.
The main disagreement that Paul has with his Jewish conversation
partner, however, is that Paul thinks his interlocutor fails at this
task![29] Indeed, Paul flatly accuses his dialogue partner of dishon-
oring God by forcing Gentiles to live in accordance with the law.
Nonetheless, later in the same letter Paul will quite forcefully
remind his Gentile audience in Rome of the irrevocable privileges
that belong to the Jewish people (see Rom 9:4-5; 11:13-24). Indeed,
Paul reminds his Gentile listeners that they are nothing more than

---

[28] Stanley K. Stowers, *A Rereading of Romans: Justice, Jews, and Gentiles* (New Haven:
Yale University Press, 1994), 145.

[29] Ibid., 126–58.

a wild olive shoot grafted into the cultivated olive tree that is historic, ethnic Israel (Rom 11:17-24).

My point in all these reflections is that Paul exhibits in Romans —and elsewhere in his letters—a consistently custodial stance towards his Gentile audience. As the influential Pauline scholar Krister Stendahl once wryly noted, in Paul's eyes a Gentile Christ follower was essentially an honorary Jew![30] It is important to see that this custodial stance on the part of Paul is thoroughly in keeping with his conviction that in proclaiming to Gentiles the Gospel of the crucified and raised Jewish Messiah, Paul was fulfilling the prophecy of Isaiah 42:6, which spoke of a Jewish servant bringing light to the nations: "I am the LORD, I have called you in righteousness, I have taken you by the hand and kept you; I have given you as a covenant to the people, a light to the nations." Paul apparently sees this prophecy fulfilled in what he understands as his prophetic call (see Gal 1:16) to gather in the Gentiles before the end of all things. It seems to me that something of this same custodial tone is evident in the rhetorical digression that comprises Hebrews 5:11-6:12. Hence, in company with Paul, the author labels his audience as unenlightened children (see also 12:7-11). The same stance of enlightened authority appears periodically throughout the letter, such as when the author repeatedly warns the community against the dangers of potential apostasy (3:12; 4:12; 6:4-6; 10:29-31; 12:25) and when he refers casually to his thorough knowledge of Jewish Scripture (9:5; 11:32).

It would be remiss of me at this point in the discussion if I did not briefly call attention to the historical fact that Jewish attitudes to Gentiles in the ancient world were anything but homogenous.[31] While it is certainly true that one can point to numerous Jewish texts that portray a negative assessment of Gentiles, it is also true that writers contemporaneous with Paul and the author of Hebrews frequently display more positive attitudes to Gentiles.[32] The

[30] Krister Stendahl, *Paul among Jews and Gentiles* (Minneapolis: Fortress Press, 1976), 37.

[31] See Pamela M. Eisenbaum, *Paul Was Not a Christian: The Original Message of a Misunderstood Apostle* (New York: Harper, 2009), 99–115.

[32] Ibid., 99–115.

ways in which Jews and Gentiles interacted socially and culturally in the world of antiquity were equally complex. While some Jewish groups espoused separation from Gentiles, much of the available literary evidence suggests that many ordinary Jews regularly interacted with their Gentile neighbors.[33]

While this proposal for an exclusively Gentile audience for Hebrews must remain a tentative one, I suggest that the question concerning the ethnic and religious identity of the audience of Hebrews is important to consider for future interpretation of Hebrews. Admittedly, the issue of the place of Gentiles in God's plan is nowhere explicitly addressed in Hebrews, as it is, for example, in several of the letters of Paul. That said, potentially fruitful avenues of interpretation arise when one views Hebrews with a Gentile audience in mind. For example, it seems to me that the focus one finds in Hebrews on the abrogation of sin accomplished by the heavenly priesthood of Jesus (see 9:26) might appear in a fresh light were we to regard this claim as addressed to an audience of Gentiles who were conscious that they did not have at their disposal the means of atonement available to Jews as prescribed by Torah.[34] In a similar light, how might a community comprised exclusively of Gentiles have resonated with the emphasis that one finds in the central section of Hebrews concerning the figure of Abraham? We know from such texts as Matthew's gospel (Matt 1:1), as well Paul's Letter to the Galatians and his Letter to the Romans (See Gal 3:6-9; Rom 4:1-12), that the figure of Abraham could function as a symbol of inclusivity, uniting both Jew and Gentile. Indeed, it is important to recall that, according to the biblical narrative, Abraham was a Gentile prior to God's call (Gen 12:1-4), a call that made of him both the father of the Jewish people and the hope of the nations. Perhaps this vision of inclusivity comprises at least part of what Hebrews is driving at when, at the conclusion of the list of Jewish heroes in chapter eleven, the author notes that these supreme Jewish exemplars of faith were not made perfect or complete apart from us (11:40), namely: a Gentile audience.

[33] Ibid., 115.
[34] Ibid., 220–22.

The Destination and Date of Hebrews

The two most popular candidates for the destination of Hebrews remain either Jerusalem or Rome. The former is the more traditional destination favored since antiquity, while the Roman proposal is increasingly advocated in contemporary Hebrews scholarship.[35] The author's preoccupation with various Jewish sacrificial rituals (see 9:13, 19-21), in addition to the status of the Levitical priesthood (Heb 7:11), has suggested to some that Hebrews was written for a community resident either in or near the city of Jerusalem. It should be pointed out, however, that Hebrews never refers to the Jerusalem temple, which was the supreme religious, cultural, and economic focal point of the city of Jerusalem in the first century CE. Instead, Hebrews consistently refers to the portable sanctuary that accompanied the Israelites during their sojourn in the wilderness (8:5; 9:1-8). An additional disadvantage to the Jerusalem proposal relates to the manner in which Hebrews cites the Jewish Bible. It is clear that Hebrews works from the Greek translation of the Jewish Bible, the Septuagint, which was the prevalent version of the Jewish Bible employed outside ancient Palestine. It would seem odd for a letter that is so dependent upon the Septuagint to be sent to a Jerusalem community resident within Palestine.[36]

The alternative proposal that argues for a Roman destination rests primarily on the strength of two observations. First, what is likely the earliest independent attestation of Hebrews appears in 1 Clement, a letter sent from Rome to Corinth probably near the end of the first century. First Clement demonstrates an awareness of the high priestly title for Jesus and reveals knowledge of at least a portion of the content found in Hebrews 1:4-13.[37] Second, there appears near the conclusion of Hebrews the following intriguing geographical notice: "Those from Italy send you greetings" (13:24). Considered grammatically, this passage is admittedly ambiguous,

---

[35] For an argument in support of the proposal for a Roman setting for Hebrews, see Kevin B. McCruden, *Solidarity Perfected: Beneficent Christology in the Epistle to the Hebrews*, BZNW 159 (Berlin/New York: de Gruyter, 2008), 122–32.

[36] See Koester, *Hebrews*, 49.

[37] See William L. Lane, *Hebrews*, vol. 1, WBC 47 (Waco, TX.: Word, 1991), lviii.

since the Greek text can mean either that Christians who are presently outside Italy are sending greetings back home to fellow believers living in Italy, or that Italian Christians in some unknown location are sending greetings to fellow believers in still another unknown location.[38] If one adopts the former reading, it is tempting to see the audience of Hebrews as constituting one of the multiple Christian house churches that appear to have been in place in the city of Rome by the mid-first century (see Rom 16:3-16). Suggestively, the only other place in the New Testament where the Greek phrase, "from Italy" appears is in Acts 18:2. In that passage, the phrase "from Italy" definitely indicates Rome.[39] Still, given the ambiguity of the Greek, any firm decision concerning the destination for Hebrews must remain—as also noted in the case of the intended audience of the letter—tentative.

A separate question that sometimes arises in discussions concerning the possible destination of Hebrews concerns whether Hebrews predates or postdates the fall of the temple in Jerusalem, an event that occurred in 70 CE. Particularly in the central section of the letter the author reveals a tendency to depict priestly sacrificial activity in the present tense (see esp. 9:6-10; 10:1). Indeed some insist that Hebrews 10:2 provides clear textual support that sacrificial rituals were still ongoing in the Jerusalem temple when Hebrews was written. Taken by itself, however, the author's depiction of ongoing sacrifices in 10:2 and elsewhere in the letter is ambiguous at best, since other contemporary sources written after the fall of the temple also employ the present tense when reflecting on the temple sacrificial system.[40]

Recently, Luke Timothy Johnson has renewed the argument for a pre-70 date for the writing of Hebrews. He argues that, if one combines Hebrews's silence on the temple with the insistence that the Levitical priesthood has given way to the heavenly high priesthood of Christ, then the likelihood becomes strong that the Jerusalem temple was still standing at the time of the composition of

[38] Ibid., 571.
[39] Ibid.
[40] See Attridge, *Epistle*, 8.

Hebrews. Johnson reasons that if the temple lie in ruins, one would naturally expect the author to belabor the point that a new eternal priesthood had in fact replaced the earthly office of the high priesthood that is now historically obsolete.[41] This line of reasoning is debatable. In my judgment, it is slightly more likely that Hebrews was written at a point in time after the temple in Jerusalem had already fallen. In a manner that is reminiscent of Mark's account of the temple incident (Mark 11:15-25), the portrait of the heavenly priesthood of Christ in Hebrews seems calculated to engage, at least in part, contemporary anxieties over the possibility of access to the presence of God attendant upon the loss of the temple in 70 CE. Such a reading makes better sense of those passages in the letter where the author celebrates the theme of renewed access to God made possible through the death and heavenly exaltation of Jesus (see 4:15-16; 6:18-19; 7:18; 10:19-22; 12:22-24). Indeed, one might plausibly argue that the rhetorical power of a Christology that depicts Christ as a heavenly and eternal high priest would be weakened if one could point to the continuing existence of both the Jerusalem temple and its earthly sacrificial rituals.

The Purpose of Hebrews

Somewhat less elusive than questions concerning the authorship and audience of Hebrews is the question relating to the possible purpose or occasion for which the author wrote. While Hebrews is anything but forthcoming concerning discrete issues that affected the community, several passages in the letter afford a glimpse of a community struggling to come to terms with the effects of social marginalization consequent upon conversion. Hebrews 10:32-34 is an especially important text in this regard:

> But recall those earlier days when, after you had been enlightened, you endured a hard struggle with sufferings, sometimes being publicly exposed to abuse and persecution, and sometimes being partners with those so treated. For you had compassion for those who were in prison and you cheerfully

---

[41] Johnson, *Hebrews*, 39. See also more recently, deSilva, *The Letter*, 57–58.

accepted the plundering of your possessions, knowing that you
yourselves possessed something better and more lasting.

Few passages in the New Testament depict more poignantly
what one might call the crisis of conversion as does Hebrews
10:32-34. Here it is important to recall that the first Christians were
what we might call first generation Christians. Conversion to the
belief in a Jewish Messiah sent by the one true God of Israel (see
1 Thess 1:9-10) could engender not only significant cognitive dis-
sonance in a polytheistic religious setting but also various forms
of resistance from members of the surrounding culture.[42] Although
elsewhere in the letter the author pointedly reminds the community that no one had thus far died as a result of persecution (see
12:4), apparently some among the audience could look back upon
specific experiences of persecution that were directly attendant
upon the faith commitment that they had placed in Jesus. In addition to imprisonment, apparent episodes of mob violence in the
form of illegal seizure of property seem to have occurred. Although
Hebrews 10:32-34 confirms that the persecution experienced by
the community entailed both physical and emotional duress, it is
probable that the latter was the more typical experience. Through
a very intentional choice of vocabulary the author highlights the
highly public character of the community's distress. Specifically,
the Greek noun *oneidismois* (abuse) implies public reproach and
censure while the Greek verb *theatrizomenoi* (publicly exposed)
means literally to be put on stage for all to see. Such vocabulary
confirms the impression gained from other places in the New
Testament (see Matt 5:11; 1 Thess 2:14; 1 Pet 2:12; 4:3-4) that the
persecution experienced by Christ's followers in the early decades
of the primitive Christian movement typically took the form of
demonstrations of social disdain from the wider culture.[43]

Since the author makes a point of affirming in 12:2 that Jesus
disregarded the shame associated with the cross, it is probable

---

[42] See Iutisone Salevao, *Legitimation in the Letter to the Hebrews: The Construction and Maintenance of a Symbolic Universe*, JSNTSup 219 (London: Sheffield, 2002), 136.

[43] Johnson, *Hebrews*, 269. See also deSilva, *The Letter*, 63.

that the Christian confessional claim that God honors a crucified man by raising him from the dead was met by significant expressions of public scorn. One must also remember that conversion entailed—especially for a Gentile audience—a dramatic and often publicly visible change in behavior that could provoke significant opposition from the dominant culture. The following passage from 1 Peter—a letter sometimes associated with Hebrews—illustrates an experience that may have resonated with many among Hebrews's audience: "You have already spent enough time in doing what the Gentiles like to do, living in licentiousness, passions, drunkenness, revels, carousing, and lawless idolatry. They are surprised that you no longer join them in the same excesses of dissipation, and so they blaspheme" (1 Pet 4: 3-4). Apart from its stereotypical portrait of Gentile sinfulness (see Wis 14:8-14), this passage demonstrates how the refusal to participate in common social activities inclusive of civic festivals, religious or trade associations, theatrical performances, or even athletic events, could open one to the potential risk of being labeled as a social and religious deviant. The public consequences deriving from such negative labeling could range from alienation from one's family (see Matt 10:34-36) to a severe loss of face in the wider society and ultimately the destruction of one's reputation as an honorable person. Given this painful scenario, the author's affirmation in 2:11 that Jesus "is not ashamed" to be associated with the community takes on added social, in addition to theological, significance (see also 11:16). Undoubtedly, the author realizes that many in the community are in fact struggling with feelings of shame and alienation due to their countercultural allegiance to Jesus, a figure whom many in the larger culture would have regarded as an executed and disgraced criminal. The real danger facing the community, therefore, is not the potential for relapse as much as it is the abandonment of commitment altogether due to the emotional distress attendant upon persecution.

Hebrews addresses the crisis attendant upon conversion by helping the community to interpret their trauma in creative ways. By employing in particular the athletic image of a "struggle," *athlēsin*, in 10:32, the author recasts the potentially shameful experience of persecution into a heroic display of praiseworthy endurance.[44] Much like a runner straining to reach the finish line despite fatigue (see 12:1), or a boxer going the full fifteen rounds despite cuts and bruises, the community endures its own personal test of public persecution for the sake of attaining the greater goal (10:33; see also 12:1) of heavenly existence in the presence of God (12:22-23, 28). What makes such a recasting of painful experience into something more than simply a creative exercise in rationalization is the figure of Jesus, who in his life, death, and exaltation provides for the audience a countercultural vantage point from which to view the apparent shame associated with the suffering that is attached to societal reproach and even physical assault. Jesus suffered perhaps the most humiliating and painful death possible and yet was exalted by God.

Throughout the letter the author makes it clear to the community that its members have experienced nothing that Jesus himself had not first experienced. Indeed, in solidarity with the faithful, Jesus also encountered rejection (12:3); he was tested by what he suffered (2:18); and he endured abuse (*oneidismon*) (13:13). Yet according to our author, it was precisely through such experiences of suffering that Jesus was made perfect or complete (2:10; 5:8-10) in the sense of being raised to new life as a heavenly and eternal high priest. As the community's "pioneer" (2:10; 12:2), "source of salvation" (5:9), and "forerunner" (6:20), Jesus offers to the socially marginalized members of Hebrews' audience evidence visible to the eyes of faith—and only to the eyes of faith—that their personal acquaintance with suffering does not disqualify them from the attainment of honor and glory. That this is so despite appearances to the contrary is demonstrated by the fact that Jesus attained honor and glory precisely through the suffering of death—a death that was directly consequent upon his own response of faithfulness before God: "In the days of his flesh, Jesus offered up prayers and supplications, with loud cries and tears, to the one who was able to save him from death, and he was heard for his reverent submission" (5:7-8). Jesus' own life, death, and glorification, then,

---

[44] See Koester, *Hebrews*, 464.

reveal that the potential suffering attending the living out of one's faith before God leads ultimately to glory. For this reason, the community addressed by Hebrews is called to embrace the shame and abuse that were both experienced and transfigured by Jesus, while all the while remaining confident that just as God raised Jesus to new life, so God will also lead to glory all those in the community who display a faith similar to Jesus' own (10:39). It is important to see, therefore, that while the author encourages his audience to maintain their countercultural commitment to Jesus, he does not extol suffering for the sake of suffering. Nor does the author of Hebrews encourage his audience to actively seek out persecution. Jesus once again is the model who puts the experience of suffering into its proper perspective. Jesus tastes death (2:9) as a result of his commitment to lead a life of righteousness (1:9) in obedience to the will of God (10:7). While it is impossible to know whether the author of Hebews had any direct familiarity with the gospel passion narratives, it seems likely that he shared the clear assumption illustrated in these narratives that Jesus was an innocent man who suffered unjustly. Why else would the author go to the trouble to highlight that Jesus was a Son who, in the words of Psalm 45:7, "loved righteousness and hated wickedness" (Heb 1:9)?

In the meantime, as the community waits to inherit God's kingdom (12:28), they are summoned by the author to consider their present struggles at the hands of a hostile culture not as a shameful indicator of their lack of worth but as a kind of educative discipline that will shape them into authentic members of the family of God:

> Endure trials for the sake of discipline. God is treating you as children; for what child is there whom a parent does not discipline? If you do not have that discipline in which all children share, then you are illegitimate and not his children. . . . Now, discipline always seems painful rather than pleasant at the time, but later it yields the peaceful fruit of righteousness to those who have been trained by it. (Heb 12:7-11)

In commenting on this passage, David deSilva helpfully points out how the author attempts to recast the community's experience with persecution in light of ancient philosophical and educational ideals associated with the task of character formation.[45] To the extent that education implies transformation through the application of rigorous and habitual exercises of both mind and body, pain and suffering are natural companions to the learning process. Once again, the figure of Jesus in his earthly ministry assumes paradigmatic significance in this regard. For, like the members of the community, Jesus too was a child who, according to the author of Hebrews, learned through the sufferings that he endured: "Although he was a Son, he learned obedience through what he suffered" (5:8). What is more, by being tested himself, Jesus is empowered to help other faithful members within God's family: "Because he himself was tested by what he suffered, he is able to help those who are being tested" (2:18). The path of suffering that Jesus walked ultimately ended with the risen Jesus entering God's presence and sitting at God's right hand (10:12; 12:2). Since this was Jesus' destiny, it gives the author confidence to say near the conclusion of the letter: "Let us then go to him outside the camp and bear the abuse that he endured. For here we have no lasting city, but we are looking for the city that is to come" (13:13).

[45] DeSilva, *The Letter*, 87.

Chapter 2

The Spiritual Life as Journey to Perfection

"And now here is my secret; a very simple secret: It is only with the heart that one can see rightly; what is essential is invisible to the eye."[1] I have always felt that this line from the book *The Little Prince* captures well the essential tone and content of the Letter to the Hebrews where invisible realities are understood by the author to be more real than visible ones. Thus, we have noticed that one of the central themes of the letter is that Jesus is alive and reigning at the right hand of God within a heavenly sanctuary. Jesus dwells, in other words, in the transcendent presence of God in a new and transformed manner as an eternal high priest. Renewed life in the presence of God is likewise the destiny of the faithful who look to Jesus as their source of salvation (5:9). In company with the Son, they too will one day appear before the face of God. For now, however, the community presently suffers persecution, and, much like the biblical patriarchs and matriarchs, they perceive their glorious destiny only from afar, if at all (11:13).

I have defined Christian spirituality as having its basis in the lived experience of an encounter with God as mediated through the life, death, and resurrection of Jesus. Such a definition is, of course, a statement of faith. It perhaps goes without saying that there is nothing inherent to the life and death of this particular Jewish healer and teacher from the Mediterranean world of the first century CE that in any way self-authenticates or necessitates

---

[1] Antoine de Saint-Eupéry, *The Little Prince*, trans. Katherine Woods (New York/San Diego: Harvest, 1971), 87.

the assertion that God was present in him. The response of faith perceives in Jesus, therefore, a transcendence that is invisible to objective perception.

The following analogy might help clarify the point I am trying to make here. My wife's love for me has its source in her experience of encountering in me something that few others see or could ever be led to see. This does not make her love any less authentic, but the fact that others do not share her experience suggests that declarations of love, much like declarations of faith, are highly relational and irreducibly personal in character.[2] When my wife declares her love for me she testifies to an experience that is real and therefore true. But the reality in question in this instance is not demonstrable as an objective fact. Something similar to this mystery within the realm of human relationships is given theological expression in the opening lines of the First Letter of John where the author testifies to experiencing the revelation of eternal life in the contingent humanity of Jesus (1 John 1:1-2): "We declare to you what was from the beginning, what we have heard, what we have seen with our eyes, what we have looked at and touched with our hands, concerning the word of life—this life was revealed, and we have seen it and testify to it, and declare to you the eternal life that was with the Father and was revealed to us." Although these words from 1 John testify to a powerful religious encounter, presumably others looked at Jesus and had no such encounter with the transcendent presence of God. Nevertheless, the author of 1 John is not being deceptive or delusional. The experience of encountering eternal life in Jesus is real precisely because a personal encounter has taken place.

The contemporary educator Parker Palmer offers some very helpful observations on this matter from the perspective of pedagogical theory. In his assessment of the limitations of purely objec-

---

[2] Sandra Schneiders maintains that faith statements touch on the "possible but non-necessary perception (faith) of divine self-disclosure (revelation)." For Schneiders this indicates that the phenomenon of divine revelation resides more properly in the realm of personal encounter than it does in objective assertion. See Sandra M. Schneiders, *The Revelatory Text: Interpreting the New Testament As Sacred Scripture* (New York: Harper, 1991), 49.

tive modes of knowing in modern models of education, Palmer notes that one encounters in a model of education informed by Christian spirituality "incarnate and personal truth," in place of truth as mediated solely in and through objectivity. Parker observes: "Where conventional education deals with abstract and impersonal facts and theories, an education shaped by Christian spirituality draws us toward incarnate and personal truth. In this education we come to know the world not simply as an objectified system of empirical objects in logical connection with each other, but as an organic body of personal relations and responses, a living and evolving community of creativity and compassion."[3] In my judgment, this is precisely what the author of 1 John is referring to within the realm of divine revelation.

In an analogous fashion, one encounters in Hebrews the faith assertion—itself engendered from highly personal religious experience—that Jesus is alive in a new manner (7:25; 10:12), that the Son reveals God (1:3), and that Christ has made it possible for the faithful to cultivate the presence of God in their own lives (4:16; 10:22). Neither of these assertions is obvious. Nor would I suggest that either assertion is true in any strictly demonstrable sense. Nevertheless, each of these faith claims constitutes for the author of Hebrews something of the transcendental vision that should shape the communal identity of his audience. Integral, therefore, to the rhetorical goal of Hebrews is what one might characterize as a larger pastoral goal that focuses on the transformation of the audience in light of transcendent realities perceptible to the eyes of faith alone: "Now faith is the assurance of things hoped for, the conviction of things not seen" (11:1).

Luke Timothy Johnson offers a helpful model for conceptualizing the link that connects spirituality with this goal of personal transformation in relation to a deeper transcendent source. Johnson defines Christian spirituality as entailing a progressive journey toward the goal of sanctity or perfection.[4] According to Johnson,

---

[3] Parker Palmer, *To Know as We Are Known: Education as Spiritual Journey* (San Francisco: Harper, 1983), 14.

[4] Luke Timothy Johnson, *Faith's Freedom: A Classic Spirituality for Contemporary Christians* (Minneapolis: Fortress Press, 1991), 9.

the journey to perfection that is the spiritual life never ends, since
it embraces the human project of aspiring to ever deeper conformity to the infinite Spirit of God.[5] One pursues the goal of conformity to God's Spirit by responding in freedom to the implicit, but
always hidden presence of God that pervades the entire creation.[6]
At least part of what this definition of spirituality suggests is that,
while an encounter with the transcendent presence of God constitutes the most fundamental feature of the Christian spiritual
experience, such an experience can be nurtured only when it is
lived out in concrete, lived behavior. Christian spirituality and
personal transformation, therefore, go hand in hand, as the author
himself suggests when he exhorts the community to accomplish
the will of God in their lives (11:36).

That the goal of human transformation is an essential characteristic of the spiritual vision of Hebrews is made clear by such
passages as Hebrews 10:22-25. In this passage the author encourages the members of the community to draw near to God in the
assurance that their conscience has been cleansed by the "blood
of Jesus" (10:19), namely: the sacrificial death of the Son:

> Therefore, my friends, since we have confidence to enter the
> sanctuary by the blood of Jesus, by the new and living way that
> he opened for us through the curtain (that is, through his flesh),
> and since we have a great high priest over the house of God,
> let us approach with a true heart in full assurance of faith, with
> our hearts sprinkled clean from an evil conscience and our
> bodies washed with pure water. . . . And let us consider how
> to provoke one another to love and good deeds, not neglecting
> to meet together, as is the habit of some, but encouraging one
> another, and all the more as you see the Day approaching.
> (10:19-25)

---

[5] The link between the idea of human process, on the one hand, and the infinite
character of God, on the other, is made already by Paul (see Phil 4:12-14). Such a
connection appears as well in the spirituality of the fourth century CE Cappadocian
Father, Gregory of Nyssa. See Gregory of Nyssa, *The Life of Moses*, trans., intro., and
notes, Everett Ferguson and Abraham J. Malherbe. Classics of Western Spirituality
(New York: Paulist Press, 1978), 115–16.

[6] Johnson, *Faith's Freedom*, 9.

What Hebrews rather enigmatically describes as the assurance of a cleansed conscience (9:14; 10:2, 22) stems from the religious experience of appropriating through the response of faith the power of the death and exaltation of Jesus.[7] That this experience should lead ideally to personal transformation in terms of practical behavior is signaled by the author's concluding exhortation. In referencing love, good deeds, and communal fellowship in verse 25, our author indicates that the spiritual journey of drawing nearer to God is essentially futile if it does not engender an accompanying transformation in terms of one's ethical relationship with others in one's community. Indeed, throughout the letter the author frequently emphasizes the importance of cultivating a life of self-sacrificial service of others (6:9-10; 10:24, 33-34; 13:3). The spirituality articulated in Hebrews, therefore, is decidedly communal in nature, rather than private. Put another way, it is a vision of the sanctity of the community, and not the individual, that engages our author. Gustavo Gutiérrez offers a similar appraisal of the nature of the spiritual life as necessarily demanding a transformation of behavior when he asserts that "the initial encounter with the Lord is the starting point of a following, or discipleship. . . . It is also what we today speak of as a *spirituality*."[8]

Encountering Jesus as High Priest

If we follow the lead of both Johnson and Gutiérrez and work from the premise that one of the root metaphors associated with

---

[7] Paul captures the dynamism of the response of faith in the following passage from Romans: "But now, apart from law, the righteousness of God has been disclosed, and is attested by the law and the prophets, the righteousness of God through faith in Jesus Christ for all who believe. For there is no distinction, since all have sinned and fall short of the glory of God; they are now justified by his grace as a gift, through the redemption that is in Christ Jesus, whom God put forward as a sacrifice of atonement by his blood, effective through faith" (Rom 3:21-25). If those scholars are correct who interpret the phrase "faith in Jesus Christ" as implying the response of trust in God that the human Jesus demonstrated in his historical ministry, then the phrase "effective through faith" likely refers to the response of trust that believers demonstrate in response to the Gospel message of the crucified and raised Jesus.

[8] Gutiérrez, *We Drink*, 54.

the concept of Christian spirituality is that of a journey or following, we might naturally inquire next as to the transcendent goal
that Hebrews encourages its audience to journey toward. To rephrase this slightly, what is the nature of the vision of perfection
that animates Hebrews? Among the various transcendent realities
available to the understanding of faith, the principal one that
Hebrews invites its listeners to reflect on concerns the deeper
identity of Jesus as a perfect high priest (7:28). On the one hand,
the author of Hebrews could be confident that many of the claims
he makes about Jesus throughout the course of his sermon would
have been familiar to his audience. Highly traditional assessments
of the identity and activity of Jesus cluster especially at the beginning of Hebrews, in that section of the letter scholars designate as
the *exordium* or formal introduction.[9] By employing, for example,
the category of Jewish wisdom reflection as gleaned from such
texts as Proverbs and the book of Wisdom, the author of Hebrews
portrays Christ as the preexistent Son who makes the invisible
God tangible and immanent within the creation.[10] Likewise traditional is the author's emphasis on the liberating and sacrificial
significance of Jesus' death (1:3; 2:15; 9:26; 10:19), as well as his
application of royal, messianic imagery to Jesus (1:2, 5, 8). On the
other hand, the author bestows on Jesus more unexpected categories and titles,[11] in particular the christological category and title
of high priest. Judging from the substantial attention that the
author devotes to the topic of the high priesthood of Jesus in the
central part of the letter (8:1–10:18), it seems likely that the repre-
sentation of Jesus as a high priest was unfamiliar to the audience
and perhaps more than a little intellectually challenging as well
(see 5:11).[12]

[9] See Mitchell, *Hebrews*, 40.

[10] See Prov 8:22-30; Wis 7:25-26; John 1:1; Col 1:15.

[11] For example, "apostle" (3:1); "forerunner" (6:20); "pioneer" (2:10); "perfector,"
(12:2). The same Greek word *archēgos* underlies the last two examples.

[12] Peter T. O'Brien observes that "Hebrews seems to be building on a traditional
Christology in order to provide 'more advanced teaching concerning Christ's priest-
hood.'" See Peter T. O'Brien, *The Letter to the Hebrews*, The Pillar New Testament
Commentary (Grand Rapids: Eerdmans, 2010), 54.

At the beginning of chapter 8 the author prefaces his most sustained reflection on the theme of the eternal priesthood of Christ with the following celebratory thesis statement: "Now the main point in what we are saying is this: we have such a high priest, one who is seated at the right hand of the throne of the majesty in heavens, a minister in the sanctuary and the true tent that the Lord, and not any mortal, has set up" (8:1-2). Although numerous texts from the New Testament interpret the death of Jesus in accordance with sacrificial terminology (e.g., Matt 26:27-28; Mark 14:24; John 1:29; 10:11; Rom 3:25), Hebrews is unique in its depiction of Jesus as a high priest. While the category of priesthood was a familiar one in the context of Greco-Roman religion, Hebrews clearly derives both the category and title of priest from the literary heritage of the Jewish Bible. This being the case, it may prove helpful at this point in our discussion to outline several historical observations concerning the Jewish priesthood.

In contrast to the priestly offices and colleges found in the surrounding Greco-Roman culture, the Jewish priesthood was conceived as a hereditary system grounded in the scriptural witness to God's choice of Aaron and his sons to maintain the desert tabernacle (Exod 28:1). While the duties of the Jewish priesthood included such responsibilities as teaching and advising, the defining attribute of the priestly office centered on the duty of the priest to attend to the mediation of God on behalf of the people (see Exod 29:44-45; Heb 5:1) through the performance of sacrifice. For the peasant base that comprised the vast majority of the population in preindustrial Palestine, the daily round of sacrifices and offerings administered in the Jerusalem temple functioned to ensure the continuation of the blessing of God's presence throughout the land. Although priestly lineage by itself did not necessarily equate with elite social status, the possession of such lineage was potentially a source of great honor and prestige.[13] During the period of the historical ministry of Jesus, the office of the Jewish high

---

[13] Luke emphasizes the nobility of both Zechariah and Elizabeth, the parents of John the Baptist, by indicating their priestly lineage (Luke 1:5-6). Zechariah, however, apparently resides in the peasant dominated countryside and Luke does not supply

priest—as opposed to the office of ordinary priests—circulated among a relatively small number of powerful families; it was from the ranks of such elite persons that the representatives of the Roman Empire appointed the high priest with the expectation that he would promote the interests of Roman provincial policy. While it is true that during the period of the Roman occupation of Palestine the high priest wielded considerable political, administrative, and social power within the city of Jerusalem, the office was nevertheless widely held in suspicion among many ordinary Jews. It should not be difficult to see why. In his ostensible role as the custodian of the covenant people of God, the high priest was expected to keep alive the tradition of liberation initiated in the exodus when God liberated the Israelites from their bondage to foreign Gentile oppressors. As an appointee of Rome, however, the high priest was obliged to attend to imperial policy (see John 11:48). The situation entailed a classic example of a conflict of interest that would eventually prove disastrous for both the inhabitants of Judea and the fate of the Jerusalem temple.[14]

The interest one sees in Hebrews in the office of the Jewish high priesthood is less informed, however, by historical observations such as these, than it is by the idealized portrait of the priesthood found in the Jewish Bible (see 5:1; 7:13-14; 9:6-7). Hence, Hebrews affirms both the hereditary status of the priestly office (7:13-14) as well as the scriptural notice that it was God who bestowed the office of the priesthood on Aaron (5:4). Of the various duties associated with the priesthood, Hebrews devotes the bulk of its attention to the role of the high priest as a mediator between God and the people. While demonstrating a familiarity with a broad range of Jewish sacrificial rituals, the author of Hebrews shows an especially keen interest in the scriptural account of the annual ritual of the Day of Atonement (see esp. 9:7, 25). It was during this

---

the reader with any other information to suggest that Zechariah and Elizabeth were socially privileged.

[14] See the discussion in Herzog, *Prophet and Teacher*, 45–46. See also Martin Goodman, *The Ruling Class of Judea: The Origin of the Jewish Revolt against Rome A.D. 66–70* (Cambridge: Cambridge University Press, 1987).

particular religious festival that the Jewish high priest would enter the most interior section of the desert sanctuary—and much later the innermost room of the Jerusalem temple—to atone annually for the collective sins of the people before the invisible presence of God (see Lev 16:1-19).

While the topic of the high priesthood of Jesus makes its first appearance in 2:17 when the author describes Jesus as both a "merciful" and "faithful high priest," it is not until chapter 7 where we see Hebrews drawing an explicit connection between the concepts of perfection and priesthood: "Now if perfection had been attainable through the Levitical priesthood—for the people received the law under this priesthood—what further need would there have been to speak of another priest arising according to the order of Melchizedek, rather than one according to the order of Aaron" (7:11)? Near the conclusion of this same chapter the author once more links the themes of perfection and priesthood: "For the law appoints as high priests those who are subject to weakness, but the word of the oath, which came later than the law, appoints a Son who has been made perfect forever" (7:28). Clearly for our author the most important thing to understand about the deeper identity of Jesus is not simply that Jesus is a high priest but that Jesus is a perfect high priest (7:28). Indeed, it is difficult to imagine how the author of Hebrews could think otherwise, since elsewhere in the letter he portrays the Son as "exalted above the heavens" (7:26) and as presently "seated at the right hand of the throne of the Majesty in the heavens" (8:1). Such remarks serve to illustrate what functions as one of the most distinctive christological convictions encountered in Hebrews—namely, that Jesus possesses a quality hitherto nonexistent among human high priests. But what precisely is this quality or attribute according to the author that sets the Son apart from ordinary high priests?

At this point in our analysis of the priestly Christology of Hebrews it is important to give some attention to the attribute of weakness that our author associates with the human high priests who are descended from Aaron. Included in the author's list of qualifications for the high priesthood (5:1-2) is the curious mention of "weakness" (*astheneian*), an attribute that the author associates with the propensity of the human high priest to commit sin: "He is able to deal gently with the ignorant and wayward, since he himself is subject to weakness; and because of this he must offer sacrifice for his own sins as well as for those of the people" (5:2-3). The appearance of the theme of weakness in 5:2 serves a larger rhetorical goal, however, since the term appears later in the context of the author's argument concerning the superior priesthood of Christ according to the order of Melchizedek (7:1-28).[15] In that section of the letter (7:15-28), weakness is no longer associated with sin but with the susceptibility to death that all human high priests must experience (7:23-28). The author's intention in widening the definition of weakness in this way becomes evident in 7:23-24, where the author asserts that unlike the human high priests descended from Aaron, Jesus is a perfect high priest owing to the heavenly existence he was granted as a consequence of his exaltation after death: "Furthermore, the former priests were many in number, because they were prevented by death from continuing in office; but he holds his priesthood permanently, because he continues forever" (7:23-24). The same thinking is apparent earlier in the chapter where we discover that the basis of Jesus' perfect priesthood lies not in priestly descent (7:14) but "through the power of an indestructible life" (7:16).

The perceptive reader may sense in these reflections a curious tension in the thought of Hebrews. Given that Hebrews designates Jesus as "sinless" (4:15) in addition to "holy," "blameless," "undefiled," and "separated from sinners" (7:26), what might our author mean when he affirms elsewhere in the letter that Jesus was made perfect or complete (2:10; 5:9; 7:28)? Unless all these

---

[15] The mysterious figure of Melchizedek appears only twice in the Jewish Bible in Genesis 14:18-20 and Psalm 110:4. Since Melchizedek functions as a kind of heavenly, angelic figure in some later Jewish texts, it is possible that the author thought him to be a particularly evocative symbol for the cosmic status that he so readily associates with the high priesthood of Jesus. At the same time, Hebrews clearly states that Melchizedek resembles the Son, not the other way round (see 7:3). See the fine discussion on possible points of contact between Jewish reflection on Melchizedek and the priestly Christology of Hebrews in Eric F. Mason, "Cosmology, Messianism, and Melchizedek: Apocalyptic Jewish Traditions and Hebrews," in *Reading the Epistle*, 53–76.

honorifics are to be ascribed to Jesus' heavenly existence, they would seem to imply that Jesus was never at any moment of his life imperfect or incomplete. I suggest that a potential way to resolve this apparent impasse is to understand these appellations as functioning to inscribe Hebrews's commentary on the distinctive shape of Jesus' life during his earthly ministry. Recall that at the beginning of this chapter I broadened the definition of spirituality to include the idea of a journey or path to perfection. I also made the observation that the spiritual journey of Christian discipleship necessarily entails the task of progressive human transformation. With these observations in mind, I propose that a hallmark of the spirituality of Hebrews resides in its portrayal of Jesus as the Son of God who progressed in his own personal journey of ever deepening conformity to the will of God. Guided by the provocative claim that Jesus himself was made perfect (2:10; 5:9; 7:28), Hebrews invites its audience to envision the process in which Jesus embodied in concrete behavior his own personal experience of an encounter with God. With this proposal as my guide, I intend to demonstrate in the remainder of this chapter how the author's distinctive vision of Jesus being made perfect functions chiefly to comment on the human response of the fidelity or faithfulness of Jesus that he demonstrated before God during his earthly ministry. The spirituality of Hebrews is, therefore, profoundly Christocentric, since the human Jesus appears in this letter as the first human being to embark on a path that leads to an encounter with God in all its potential fullness: "We have this hope, a sure and steadfast anchor of the soul, a hope that enters the inner shrine behind the curtain, where Jesus, a forerunner on our behalf, has entered" (6:19-20).

The Perfection of Jesus: Preliminary Reflections

The scholarly investigation of Hebrews has witnessed something of a reevaluation of traditional attempts at interpreting the letter. While much speculation in the past focused on locating a single conceptual background to the letter, more recently there has emerged an increasing appreciation for how Hebrews likely employs multiple conceptual models for the crafting of its rich Christology.[16] Indeed, the author appears particularly skilled at blending numerous intellectual backgrounds, in particular platonic categories and apocalyptic motifs. Particularly welcome of late has been the recognition of the narrative character of the theology contained in many of the writings of the New Testament.[17] Such a turn to the text raises renewed possibilities for the task of drawing fruitful connections between the narrative world of Hebrews and its Christology of Christ perfected.

In what follows I intend to analyze the idea of the perfection of Jesus in Hebrews while guided by the methodological assumption that a larger narrative world or theological story informs this ancient sermon. James C. Miller defines the conceptual category of a narrative world as a "component" of a culturally conceived symbolic universe. If one thinks of a symbolic universe as the aggregate of the conceptual lenses through which one interprets reality, then a narrative world refers more explicitly to the deepest personal assumptions, convictions, and aspirations associated with that symbolic world.[18] While the author of Hebrews could expect the majority of his auditors to find many of the aspects of its story world familiar, this same narrative world will likely strike contemporary readers as profoundly alien. In this story world, for example, God appears as the transcendent source of life and the One for whom judgment will be reserved at the end of time (2:10; 4:13; 9:27; 10:30-31). Likewise, sin in the story world of Hebrews functions as a barrier impeding access to God and can only be removed through the act of sacrificial expiation (1:3; 9:14, 22, 26;

[16] Kenneth Schenck, *Cosmology and Eschatology in Hebrews: The Settings of the Sacrifice*, SNTSS 143 (Cambridge: Cambridge University Press, 2007), 5.

[17] Schenck, *Cosmology*, 13. A pioneering work in the application of narrative categories to the epistolary texts of the New Testament can be found in Richard B. Hays, *The Faith of Jesus Christ: An Investigation of the Narrative Substructure of Galatians 3:1–4:11* (Chico, CA: Scholars Press, 1983).

[18] See James C. Miller, "Paul and Hebrews: A Comparison of Narrative Worlds," in *Hebrews: Contemporary Methods—New Insights*, ed. Gabriela Gelardini, Biblical Interpretation Series 75 (Leiden: Brill, Repr., Atlanta: Society of Biblical Literature, 2008), 246–47.

10:12, 14). Perhaps most alien of all to our modern sensibilities is the letter's valorization—quite typical of the ancient world—of unseen, eternal reality as fundamentally more real than perceptible reality (8:1-5; 9:11, 23-24).

I do not intend to examine every facet of the theological story of Hebrews. Instead, this chapter will focus largely on the human career of Jesus within the narrative world of Hebrews, in particular the role that perfection occupies in the human career of Jesus. I share the opinion that Hebrews reveals an affinity with the theological perspective taken on the shape of the Christ event as depicted in the so-called *kenosis* hymn found in Paul's Letter to the Philippians (2:6-11).[19] The frequent emphasis one sees in Hebrews concerning the exaltation of Jesus into the presence of God as a consequence of suffering and death (1:3; 5:8-10; 7:26-28; 10:12-13) conforms to the similar pattern of humiliation followed by exaltation, discernible in the *kenosis* hymn contained in Philippians. In a manner reminiscent of the opening verse of that hymn (Phil 2:6), where Jesus is described as being in the form of God, the *exordium* of Hebrews (1:1-4) begins by depicting the glorified Son in accordance with the category of Jewish Wisdom (1:3). Echoing in particular the description of personified Wisdom found in Wisdom 7:25, the author of Hebrews depicts the glorified Jesus as the "reflection" (*apaugausma*) of God's glory. Despite references in the opening part of the letter to what we might call the incarnation beginning in 2:14-18, much of the body of Hebrews focuses on what the *kenosis* hymn in Philippians describes as Jesus' self-emptying (Phil 2:7), namely, Jesus' earthly career and in particular his high priestly activity that culminates in sacrificial death. In contrast to the *kenosis* hymn, however, Hebrews eschews the metaphor of slavery (Phil 2:7) in favor of developing the theme of the radical solidarity that Jesus enters into with humanity (2:14, 18; 4:15), a solidarity that culminates in the author's distinctive vision of Christ as both victim and priest (9:26). Lastly, the *kenosis* hymn concludes on the triumphal note of Jesus' resurrection, conceived along the lines of cosmic exaltation (Phil 2:9-11). Similarly, the

---

[19] See Miller, "Paul and Hebrews," 261.

author of Hebrews consistently celebrates throughout his extended theological exposition a portrait of the glorified Jesus as
the living and reigning Son, who fulfills the scriptural vision of
Ps 110:1: "The LORD says to my lord, 'Sit at my right hand until I
make your enemies your footstool.'"

Hebrews's reflections concerning the perfection of Jesus relate
essentially to the second and third stages of the human career of
Jesus as outlined above. On the one hand, perfection for Jesus, as
well as for the believer, involves the event of exaltation or glorification into the eternal presence of God. Hebrews describes this
end time destiny of encounter with the divine presence with a
variety of fresh metaphors that serve to nurture the eschatological
hopes of its audience: participation in a heavenly calling (3:1);
entering into Sabbath rest (4:9); approaching the "throne of grace"
(4:16); arrival at the heavenly Jerusalem (12:22); and perhaps most
evocatively, stepping behind the curtain of the heavenly sanctuary
to encounter God (6:19; 10:19). While the author is confident that
Jesus has already attained the goal of entering into the presence
of God (1:6; 10:12-13), for the faithful such communion with God
is ultimately a heavenly destiny whose final fulfillment lies in the
age to come (12:28; 13:14).

As we will see in the next chapter, however, the author of Hebrews can at the same time conceive of communion with God as
in some sense a present reality that has been made possible
through the death and exaltation of Jesus. On the other hand, the
perfection of Jesus in Hebrews has as much to do with the response of faithfulness that the human Jesus demonstrated during
his public ministry. Jesus is, for example, the faithful Son whose
response of faithfulness surpasses that of Moses (3:1-2). Jesus is
also the obedient Son, who through his exemplary obedience
demonstrated piety before God (5:7-9; 10:5-9). Indeed, fundamental to the Christology of Hebrews is the idea that the experiences
of suffering endured by Jesus tested him and thereby demonstrated his fitness both to be God's Son and ultimately a heavenly
advocate for human beings (2:18; 4:15). The faithfulness of the
Son—which according to our author was made complete through
Jesus' acceptance of suffering and death on behalf of embodying

God's kingdom—in turn models for believers the faithfulness that is to characterize their own lives as they, too, embark on the journey to perfection (see 12:2; 13:21).

The Perfection of Jesus:
Jesus as the Representative Human Being

Few texts in the New Testament offer a more theologically complex appraisal of the Christ event than the Letter to the Hebrews. Fewer still cultivate the concept of perfection as deliberately as does Hebrews in working out the implications of Christ's death for both the person of Jesus and the identity of the believer.[20] Nevertheless, it is difficult to arrive at a clear understanding of the idea of perfection in Hebrews since abundant comparative material from the ancient world exists that provides a diverse range for the application of perfection terminology. And it is doubtful that Hebrews adopts any of these usages in any kind of arbitrary fashion.[21]

The author of Hebrews applies perfection terminology directly to Jesus three times in the letter (2:10, 5:9; 7:28). In each instance the author employs the same Greek verb *teleioō*. At the most basic lexical level, *teleioō* denotes the formal concept of completion in the sense of attaining a goal.[22] Since in practice, however, ancient writers made use of the verb in a variety of ways, one must examine the surrounding literary context to discern the specific nuance of completion that a given author has in view. For example, the verb appears in the writings of the Jewish philosopher Philo of Alexandria to describe both the maturation of a harvest (*Praem.* 128) and the completion of a specific task (*Opif.* 89). The verb could also be used metaphorically to refer to the termination of life, as when the author of 4 Maccabees praises the heroic death of the

---

[20] Although sometimes obscured by English translations, perfection terminology appears in the following passages of Hebrews: 2:10; 3:14; 5:9, 14; 6:1, 8, 11; 7:3, 11, 19, 28; 9:9, 11; 10:1, 14; 11:40; 12:2, 23.

[21] Attridge, *Epistle*, 86.

[22] See Koester, *Hebrews*, 122–23.

Jewish martyr, Eleazar, who endures physical persecution for his refusal to eat ritually defiled food (4 Macc 7:15; see also Philo, *Leg.* 3:45). The author of the third gospel also seems to be conscious of this connection between death and perfection, since Luke can equate the goal of Jesus' ministry with his impending prophetic death in Jerusalem (Luke 13:32-33). In a similar way, John's gospel uses a Greek verb derived from the same *tel*-root (*tetelestai*) to describe the moment preceding Jesus' death on the cross (John 19:30). This latter use of the terminology of perfection is especially suggestive given the supreme emphasis we encounter in Hebrews on the suffering and death of Jesus.

The verb *teleioō* could also convey more specifically religious associations, as when both Plato and Philo employ the verb in reference to the initiation rites of the mystery religions (Philo, *Mos.* 2.14; Plato, *Phaed.* 249C). Several passages in the Septuagint employ the verb in this specifically religious sense to describe persons who demonstrate faithfulness to God, especially through their display of ethical righteousness (Sir 31:10; Wis 4:13-14). Interestingly, the author of Hebrews also makes a point of emphasizing the righteousness of Jesus in his royal capacity as Messiah (1:9). In addition, in 7:2 the author supplies his listeners with the following etymological observation concerning the name Melchizedek: "His name, in the first place, means, 'king of righteousness.'" Since the author makes a point of saying in 7:3 that Melchizedek resembles the Son, it follows that righteousness is a quality that the author understands to be embodied by Jesus. In a more philosophical vein, Philo frequently employs perfection terminology in order to conceptualize the act of contemplation, as well as the life of virtue that promotes the contemplative ascent of the mind above the senses (*Leg.* 3.74; *Sacr.* 120). In the New Testament, Paul construes perfection in a religious sense when he describes the mystical goal of his life as a "straining forward" to live in conformity to the pattern of Christ's suffering and resurrection (Phil 3:10-13). Outside of Hebrews, *teleioō* appears most frequently in the New Testament in the Fourth Gospel (John 4:34; 5:36), where it is used to depict Jesus as the Son who brings to completion the will or commission of God.

While this broad rehearsal of the conceptual background of perfection language is helpful for historically contextualizing Hebrews within its ancient setting, clues for interpreting the meaning of the concept of perfection as applied to Jesus in Hebrews are best gained by giving close attention to the surrounding literary contexts in which the verb appears. With this exegetical principle in mind, we read the following in Hebrews 2:10: "It was fitting that God, for whom and through whom all things exist, in bringing many children to glory, should make the pioneer of their salvation perfect through sufferings." Two items in this verse should immediately capture our attention. First, the author carefully links the idea of the perfection of Jesus with the sufferings that Jesus experienced (see also 2:9; 5:8-9). Second, Hebrews envisions the completion of Jesus as connected in some manner to the divine intention to lead the "many children to glory" (2:10).[23] For the author of Hebrews, then, the destiny of Jesus has implications for the destiny of humankind as well. The occurrence of the words "glory" and "sufferings" in 2:10 should be read in close proximity with the material that immediately precedes it in 2:5-9:

> Now God did not subject the coming world, about which we are speaking, to angels. But someone has testified somewhere, "What are human beings that you are mindful of them, or mortals, that you care for them? You have made them for a little while lower than the angels; you have crowned them with glory and honor, subjecting all things under their feet." Now in subjecting all things to them, God left nothing outside their control. As it is, we do not yet see everything in subjection to them, but we do see Jesus, who for a little while was made lower than the angels, now crowned with glory and honor because of the suffering of death, so that by the grace of God he might taste death for everyone.

---

[23] Here the NRSV correctly translates the intention behind the Greek of Hebrews which speaks literally of God leading the "many sons" (*huious*) "to glory." The author obviously assumes a broader audience for his sermon than just males.

Whether it is accurate to view Hebrews 2:5-9 as functioning as a kind of thesis statement for the entire letter,[24] this passage is certainly important for what it reveals about our author's understanding of the deeper identity of Jesus. Prior to this section of the letter, the author celebrates the cosmic status that the Son presently occupies as a result of being raised to new life (1:1-2:4). Jesus is the Son in whom God has definitely spoken (1:2); the Son is, moreover, the "reflection of God's glory" (1:3) and even played a mediating role in the creation of the cosmos (1:2). Above all else, the author assures his audience that the risen Jesus has entered into the heavenly world where God dwells (1:6).[25] Beginning in 2:5 and extending through 2:18, however, the focus of Hebrews noticeably switches to the earthly ministry of Jesus.[26] This section of the letter begins with a subtle echo—unfortunately lost in English translation—to one of the principal themes announced earlier in the exordium—namely, the existence of a heavenly realm that exists beyond the region of earthly existence. This transcendent realm is where ultimately reality exists according to the author of Hebrews. Hence, in 1:6 we read that God "leads" (*eisagagē*) Jesus, the "first-born" (*prōtotokon*) into this "world" (*oikoumenēn*), whereupon the Son is immediately worshipped by the angels. Since the author consistently makes use of the Greek noun *kosmos* when he wishes to designate the realm of human existence (see 10:5; 11:7, 38), it is evident that the "world" envisioned in 1:6 is of a different character, namely, a heavenly world.[27] The author further amplifies

---

[24] See Koester, *Hebrews*, 219–20.

[25] Although one hesitates, given the complexity of the theological reflection contained in Hebrews, to privilege a single theme as primary, the following verse certainly captures a consistent emphasis in the letter: "For Christ did not enter a sanctuary made by human hands, a mere copy of the true one, but he entered into heaven itself, now to appear in the presence of God on our behalf" (9:24).

[26] Frank Matera notes: "Having established the superiority of the Son through this Christological exegesis, in the second exposition (2:5-18) Hebrews turns its attention to the abasement of the Son." See Frank J. Matera, "The Theology of the Epistle to the Hebrews," in *Reading the Epistle*, 194.

[27] Hebrews likewise appraises the sanctuary located in heaven as qualitatively superior to the earthly (*kosmikon*) sanctuary. The author makes a point of affirming that Christ entered the former and not the latter (9:24).

the heavenly nature of this world both by the notice in 1:3 that the Son is seated "at the right hand of the Majesty on high," and by the claim in 1:6 that God commanded the angels to worship the exalted Jesus. The Greek word *oikoumenēn* appears for the second and final time in Hebrews in 2:6; only now the author describes the *oikoumenēn* as "the world (*oikoumenēn*) to come." The inference to be drawn from these observations seems clear: Hebrews strikingly claims that the heavenly region first entered by Jesus is also the divinely intended dwelling place for the socially beleaguered listeners of his sermon. Indeed, the heavenly realm that Jesus entered following his death and exaltation is none other the place of "glory" (*doxan*) that God is presently leading (*agagonta*) the children toward (2:10). The author provides his listeners with a suggestive hint of this transcendent reality near the conclusion of chapter 12: "This phrase, 'Yet once more,' indicates the removal of what is shaken—that is, created things—so that what cannot be shaken may remain. Therefore, since we are receiving a kingdom that cannot be shaken, let us give thanks" (12:27-28).

The theme of glory as the heavenly destiny for the children of God serves as the interpretive key for the author's selection and analysis of Psalm 8 in 2:6-8. Hebrews closely follows the wording of the psalm as it appears in the Septuagint.[28] In terms of its setting in both the Hebrew Bible and the Septuagint, Psalm 8 celebrates the preeminent position that humanity presently occupies in the creation. To that end, the psalm pictures human beings as having the glory and honor that derives from exercising dominion over the realm of creation (see Psalm 8:6-8). The theme of dominance over the creation is particularly evident in the original Hebrew of the psalm, which depicts human beings as possessing a nature that ranks just beneath that of the angels (Psalm 8:5). Hebrews engages in what we might call a creative "re-scripturing" of Psalm

---

[28] Hebrews leaves out, however, verse 6: "You have given them dominion over the works of your hands," which appears in both the Septuagint and MT of the Hebrew Bible. The author's clear dependence on the Septuagint is demonstrated by 2:7, where he closely follows the Septuagint translation "angels" (*angelois*) for the original Hebrew *elohîm* (Psalm 8:5), which could mean either God or angels.

8 in three important ways. First, by relying upon the Greek translation found in the Septuagint, the author interprets the lowering
of humanity as a temporal as opposed to an ontological lowering.
"You have made them for a little while lower than the angels"
(Heb 2:7). This temporal reading has the effect of insinuating in
the minds of the listeners that humanity's stature—at least according to the divine intention—is actually superior to that of the
angels.[29] Second, while retaining the theme present in the psalm
concerning the subjection of the creation to humanity (2:8), the
author performs the crucial exegetical move of interpreting such
sovereignty as a reality that does not, in fact, presently exist. This
last observation bears repeating. Hebrews pointedly denies that
all things are, at present, subject to humanity: "Now in subjecting
all things to them, God left nothing outside their control. As it is,
we do not yet see everything in subjection to them" (2:8). This
denial of the supremacy of humanity in relation to the creation
suggests, in turn, that the reference to God crowning humanity
with glory and honor (2:7) must also function as a yet unrealized
promise. All this makes sense given that the author has already
hinted that the salvation to be inherited (1:14) pertains to the transcendent world that is to come (2:5). Third, and perhaps most
importantly in light of the Christology of Hebrews, the author
understands the generic human being of Psalm 8 to refer to Jesus,
who is the first human being to bring to realization the divine
intention for humanity's universal, cosmic sovereignty:[30] "But we
do see Jesus, who for a little while was made lower than the angels,
now crowned with glory and honor" (2:9). The outcome of our
author's creative appropriation of Psalm 8 is that the psalm no

[29] The superiority of human beings to the angelic creation is tacitly implied in 1:14,
where the angels serve a ministering function for those whom God intends to save.
[30] David Moffitt makes the intriguing claim that the exalted Jesus functions in
Hebrews as the first glorified human being to enter the heavenly sanctuary. Hebrews
clearly understands the embodied existence of Jesus as playing a central role in the
Son's entrance into the heavenly sphere (see 5:7-8; 9:26; 10:19-20). It seems to me that
Hebrews is less clear, however, about the precise nature of Jesus' embodied existence
after the event of the Son's exaltation. See David M. Moffitt, "Unveiling Jesus' Flesh:
A Fresh Assessment of the Relationship between the Veil and Jesus' Flesh in Hebrews
10:20," in *Perspectives in Religious Studies* 37 (2010): 84.

longer functions as a celebration of humanity's present grandeur. Instead, the author interprets psalm 8 as referring to the heavenly destiny that God intends for human beings to enter in the future. This is a destiny that, according to the author of Hebrews, became a potential reality in the person of Jesus, who was the first to enter the heavenly *oikoumenēn*. Those scholars are likely correct, therefore, who contend that the concept of Jesus' perfection in Hebrews should in the first instance be viewed in light of the connection that our author draws between perfection and exaltation into the heavenly realm: "For Christ did not enter a sanctuary made by human hands, a mere copy of the true one, but he entered into heaven itself, now to appear in the presence of God on our behalf" (9:24). On this issue, the following observation by John Scholer is representative of many commentators: "The parallel drawn in 2:9-10 suggests that Jesus' being 'crowned with glory and honor' (2.9) corresponds to his 'being brought to perfection' (2.10). . . . To consider that God has led Jesus to the goal is therefore to understand his 'perfection' as his 'glorification' or 'entry' into the heavenly holy of holies."[31] Jesus is perfected, in other words, when God raises the human Jesus to new and everlasting life in the heavenly world: "But when Christ came as a high priest of the good things that have come, then through the greater and perfect tent (not made with hands, that is, not of this creation), he entered once for all into the Holy Place" (9:11-12).

A Body You Have Prepared for Me: The Faithfulness of Jesus

Apart from a brief reference at the beginning of the exordium to the expiatory effect of the sacrificial death of Jesus (1:3), Hebrews gives little attention in the first chapter and a half of the

---

[31] John M. Scholer, *Proleptic Priests: Priesthood in the Epistle to the Hebrews*, JSNTSup 49 (Sheffield: JSOT, 1991), 195–96. See also Marie Isaacs, *Sacred Space: An Approach to the Theology of the Epistle to the Hebrews*, JSNTSup 73 (Sheffield: Sheffield Academic, 1992), 44; Ernst Käsemann, *The Wandering People of God: An Investigation of the Letter to the Hebrews*, trans. Roy A. Harrisville and Irving L. Sandberg (Minneapolis: Augsburg, 1984), 40.

sermon to the memory of the passion of Jesus. This changes, however, beginning in 2:9, when the author dramatically depicts Jesus as having tasted death on behalf of everyone, and as having been invested with glory and honor precisely as a consequence of the experience of suffering and death. As if to further underscore the importance that the passion holds for the perfecting of Jesus, the author goes on to propose that it was appropriate or "fitting" for God to bring Jesus to completion in this manner (2:10). What accounts for this sudden transition to a theme of the humility of Jesus' human career?

At least a partial answer to this question resides in the avowed pastoral purpose of Hebrews as a "word of exhortation" (13:22). As I have already noted in the previous chapter, Hebrews supplies an affecting window into an early Christian community struggling with the painful social and psychological effects of social marginalization (see esp. 10:32-34; 12:4; 13:13). It would have been difficult in the extreme for a community subjected to the kind of societal reproach and derision evident in such passages as 10:32-34 to see anything remotely akin to glory or honor in their collective struggle with persecution. Behind the summons to the community in 12:12 to "lift drooping hands and strengthen your weak knees" lies the author's awareness that feelings of shame and discouragement likely affected many in the community as a result of such harassment. In order to respond, therefore, to the potential for significant communal malaise,[32] the author employs in 2:9-18 a Christology that functions in large part to address the trauma attendant upon the experience of persecution. Given that Jesus experienced in his own ministry both the animosity of enemies (12:3) as well as the physical and emotional degradation of crucifixion (12:2), the community's experience of being labeled social deviants becomes capable of being viewed in a different light. Indeed, the author would have his audience understand that Jesus entered the heavenly *oikoumenēn* precisely as a consequence of enduring the painful experience of humiliating suffering and death. Since

---

[32] It is possible that the failure of some in the community to assemble for fellowship is connected to feelings of discouragement in the face of persecution (see 10:25).

this same Jesus took "his seat at the right hand of God" (12:2), the community can expect the same heavenly reward (10:35) provided they persevere (10:35-39; 12:7-11), just as Jesus did (12:2). The pastoral program of Hebrews becomes especially evident in those passages where the author insists that Jesus "tasted death" by means of God's grace (2:9) and that the sufferings experienced by Jesus were in some way appropriate or fitting for bringing to fulfillment the divine intention (2:10). By closely relating in this manner the suffering and death of Jesus to the providential purpose of God to lead the "many children to glory," Hebrews seeks to transform the potentially debilitating effects of persecution into something more theologically and existentially meaningful for his audience.[33]

The author's evident awareness of significant levels of communal distress likely also accounts for the emphasis one sees in chapter 2 on the motif of Jesus' solidarity with humanity.[34] The theme of solidarity is first announced in 2:11, where the author maintains that "the one who sanctifies and those who are sanctified all have one Father." Although this verse is ambiguous in terms of the original Greek, the thought expressed seems to be that both Jesus (the sanctifier) and all of humanity (the sanctified) have their origin in God.[35] Having in this way established the theme of solidarity as a general principle, the author proceeds to draw out the deeper implications of the fraternal bond that links the listeners with the Son.[36] In a striking passage that allows the audience to overhear the voice of Jesus speaking directly to God, Jesus describes the children destined for glory as the children given to the Son by God (2:13). The description of the incarnation

---

[33] Koester observes: "The exaltation that followed Jesus' passion gives listeners confidence that their own suffering is not the final word, but part of the way in which God is bringing them to glory." Koester, *Hebrews*, 236.

[34] For a detailed discussion of this topic see Kevin B. McCruden, "Christ's Perfection in Hebrews: Divine Beneficence as an Exegetical Key to Hebrews 2:10," in *BR* 47 (2002) 40–62; see also Kevin B. McCruden, "Compassionate Soteriology in Hebrews, 1 Peter, and the Gospel of Mark," in *BR* 52 (2007): 44–48.

[35] Koester, *Hebrews*, 236; Attridge, *Epistle*, 89.

[36] See Thompson, *The Beginnings*, 92; Gray, "Hebrews Among," 23–25.

of the Son that immediately follows in 2:14-18 accentuates the depth of Jesus' involvement with, and concern for, the recipients of this sermon. To that end, the author affirms that Jesus partook of the flesh and blood of the "children" (2:14),[37] and took hold not of angels, but of the seed of Abraham (2:16). The purpose of the incarnation was, on the one hand, to bring liberation to believers from the tyranny of the fear of death and, on the other hand, for the Son to be made like the many brothers and sisters, so that he might become a merciful as well as a faithful high priest (2:17). Illustrative once more of the pastoral problem attendant upon persecution, chapter 2 concludes with the encouraging reminder that since Jesus was tested during his earthly ministry, he can now in his status as the risen Lord lend assistance to the faithful as they struggle with their own challenging experiences of personal testing at the hands of a hostile culture (2:18).

By now it should be clear to the reader that the theme of the perfection of Jesus serves an important pastoral function in Hebrews. Nevertheless, it would be inaccurate to contend that Hebrews conceives of the perfection of Jesus solely in connection with the project of communal exhortation. The latter is clearly important to our author; however, a purely sociological reading of the Christology of Hebrews is ultimately inadequate since it fails to account for how the concept of perfection also functions as theological commentary on the personality of Jesus—namely, the kind of Son that Jesus is.[38] In his analysis of Hebrews 2:17, a passage that speaks qualities of mercy and faithfulness embodied by Jesus, Craig Koester offers the helpful observation that "suffering was the way that the qualities of mercy and faithfulness became evi-

---

[37] The Greek of Hebrew 2:14 might be better translated as: "Since therefore the children shared in flesh and blood, so he himself, in a similar fashion, partook of the same."

[38] Hebrews is not alone among the writings of the New Testament for showing such a concern with what we might call character analysis. The elaborate legendary accounts of the testing of Jesus found in both Matthew (4:1-11) and Luke (4:1-13) largely function to reflect theologically on the kind of Messiah Jesus will be in the context of his historical ministry.

dent in Jesus the high priest."[39] To rephrase, I suggest that fundamental to our author's priestly Christology is his assumption that the reigning Lord who ministers in the heavenly sanctuary is also the human exemplar of what the shape of the journey to perfection looks like on this side of the age to come. In other words, according to the author of Hebrews, the Son who has conquered death and has been exalted to the right hand of God is the same Jesus who embarked on his own personal journey to communion with God by aligning his spirit to the infinite spirit of God (see 9:14). The human Jesus embodies in a paradigmatic fashion the essence of the spiritual life, which as we have seen means essentially living or walking by the light of transcendent reality. Important clues, demonstrating that the motif of Jesus' human response before God is an important consideration for our author, are evident throughout the sermon. For example, while the essential point of the exordium lies in its celebration of the enthroned Son in the heavenly *oikoumenēn*, already in 1:9 the author can describe the exalted Jesus as the royal figure who, in the context of his earthly ministry, "loved righteousness" and "hated wickedness." Indeed, the author understands the royal anointing of Jesus—understood as his exaltation—as having taken place in large measure as a consequence of Jesus' commitment to live a life of righteousness. In both of these instances the author is likely thinking, at least in part, of the tradition expressed in the gospels concerning Jesus' innocence. A similar concern for the righteous response of Jesus before God appears in the notice concerning Jesus' faithfulness in 2:17. Here we note that part of the author's stated rationale for Jesus' incarnation was so that the Son might become a "faithful," as well as a "merciful high priest." We might also recall here the author's claim in 3:2 that Jesus was, like Moses, faithful to the God who appointed him. The idea of faithfulness, if not the precise term, is likewise also in view in Hebrews 12:2, a passage where the author describes Jesus as the Son who despised the shame of the cross for the sake of the joy that lie before him. The location

---

[39] Koester, *Hebrews*, 236.

in Hebrews where Jesus' response of faithful obedience before God is given its most explicit expression, however, is in 10:5-10:

> Consequently, when Christ came into the world, he said, "Sacrifices and offerings you have not desired, but a body you have prepared for me; in burnt offerings and sin offerings you have taken no pleasure. Then I said, 'See, God, I have come to do your will, O God' (in the scroll of the book it is written of me)." When he said above, "You have neither desired nor taken pleasure in sacrifices and offerings and burnt offerings and sin offerings" (these are offered according to the law), then he added, "See, I have come to do your will." He abolishes the first in order to establish the second. And it is by God's will that we have been sanctified through the offering of the body of Jesus Christ once for all.

This passage—which I will discuss in further detail in chapter 4—appears near the end of the author's extensive argument found in 8:1–10:18 concerning the superiority of the heavenly sacrifice of Jesus in comparison to the sacrifices conducted under the Levitical priesthood.[40] Two main topics afford theological coherence and structure to this section of the letter: (1) the superior location where the sacrificial activity of Jesus takes place and (2) the superior nature of Jesus' high priestly sacrifice. Spatially, Christ's sacrificial activity proves superior to the sacrificial activity of ordinary Levitical priests since it takes place in what Hebrews describes as the authentic tent or sanctuary that is located in heaven (8:1; 9:11-12) as opposed to a sanctuary located on earth (8:5; 9:1, 11): "For Christ did not enter a sanctuary made by human hands, a mere copy of the true one, but he entered into heaven itself." (9:24). Standing in the immediate background of such comments concerning a heavenly sanctuary is the scriptural account of the por-

---

[40] It is important not to draw from this comparison the erroneous conclusion that Hebrews promotes any form of supersessionism—namely, the idea that Christianity triumphs over, or is superior to, Judaism. Alan C. Mitchell demonstrates that the rhetorical tool of comparison functions in Hebrews as a way of comparing realities that the author understands as inherently excellent. See Alan C Mitchell, "A Sacrifice of Praise," in *Reading the Epistle*, 256.

table sanctuary that accompanied the Israelites during their wanderings in the wilderness (Exod 25-27). Indeed, throughout 8:1–10:18 the author is keenly interested in the link between the wilderness sanctuary and the idea of the presence of God. According to the biblical account, once the sanctuary was completed, the "glory" (*kābôd*) or presence of God filled the portable tabernacle for the purpose of accompanying the Israelites on their journey to the Promised Land (Exod 40:34-38). The importance of the theme of the presence of God is made most evident in 9:24, which states that when Jesus entered the heavenly sanctuary he came face to face with God. Hebrews also shows a marked interest in God's command to Moses to construct the sanctuary in accordance with the pattern or example revealed to him on the mountain (Exod 25:40). This scriptural detail confirms for the author that there exists an ideal sanctuary in relation to an earthly sanctuary that cannot ever be more than a humanly constructed copy of a superior heavenly reality (9:11, 23-24).

There is extensive scholarly debate over the possible conceptual background that may be influencing the author's view of a sanctuary in heaven. Some scholars point to passages such as Hebrews 8:5, which seems to make a distinction between a heavenly and an earthly sanctuary, as evidence that Hebrews is influenced by a Platonizing emphasis on transcendent reality that alone counts as fully real in comparison to the world of sense perception.[41] Other scholars have suggested that apocalyptically tinged depictions of heavenly sanctuaries and thrones described by various Jewish second temple texts might provide a better conceptual fit for the heavenly sanctuary envisioned in Hebrews.[42] However one may conceive of the appropriate background for our author's thinking—and it is likely that both backgrounds are in fact mingled

[41] See James W. Thompson, "What Has Middle Platonism to Do with Hebrews," in *Reading the Epistle*, 31–52.

[42] Without denying the likelihood that platonic categories more than likely have influenced Hebrews's thinking on this issue, Eric F. Mason makes a persuasive case that apocalyptic descriptions of heavenly sanctuaries and thrones may have played a more fundamental role in Hebrews's emphasis on Jesus' heavenly priesthood. See Mason, "Cosmology," in *Reading the Epistle*, 56–60.

in Hebrews—it seems clear that the author's primary intention is to show that Christ entered into the transcendent presence of God (8:2; 9:11-12, 24). And since in the thought world of Hebrews transcendent realities are better than earthly realities (see 9:23-24; 12:27-28), the heavenly location of Christ's sacrificial ministry (8:1-2) makes his offering superior to the sacrificial offerings that take place in any mere earthly sanctuary (8:5).

For all the obvious emphasis that Hebrews places on the spatial superiority of Jesus' priestly activity, it is just as crucial to see that Hebrews understands the superior nature of Jesus' sacrifice as arising out of its radically personal quality: Jesus is a priest, who is at once also a victim (9:26). Recall that earlier in the sermon the author recounted the qualifications for the human priesthood; included among these qualifications was the responsibility "to offer gifts and sacrifices for sins" (5:1). Hebrews depicts Jesus as a high priest who, like other human high priests, does in fact make an offering; but Jesus' offering is decidedly more experiential: namely, prayers and supplications accompanied by emotional distress (5:7). In 8:3 we once again encounter a reference to the offerings made by human priests, and once more we find a similar emphasis placed on the external character of the priestly offerings offered by ordinary priests. In place of external gifts, Jesus offers, in contrast, the gift of his own life (8:3; 9:14). Much the same thought is captured by Hebrews's repeated references to the image of Jesus' blood, an image that apparently functions for the author as a metaphor for Jesus' self-giving of his life. No less than five times in the space of two chapters, the author makes the point that the blood offered by priests and even Moses was not their own. By contrast, when Jesus entered the heavenly sanctuary he gave his own blood (9:7, 12, 19, 25; 10:4).

This emphasis on the personal quality of Jesus' sacrificial activity shows that, while the idea of exaltation to glory constitutes one aspect of what it means for the Son to be perfected, the language of perfection also encompasses the earthly career of Jesus and in particular the response of faithfulness on the part of Jesus. In an important study devoted to the concept of perfection in Hebrews, David Peterson proposes a vocational understanding of the concept. According to Peterson, Jesus' perfection entails "a whole sequence of events" that, while including Jesus' exaltation, is not limited to the Son's entry into the heavenly sphere.[43] Crucial to Peterson's argument is his insistence that the event of the suffering and death of Jesus functions in Hebrews as something more than just a preliminary stage for Jesus' subsequent glorification. Instead, the experience of suffering and death serves as part of a larger experiential process that culminates in the exaltation of the Son.[44] While it would be incorrect to say that Hebrews thinks of such an experiential process along the lines of moral development within the person of Jesus, it is appropriate to affirm that Hebrews thinks of the human Jesus as growing or maturing in some way in the context of his human career.[45] An adequate interpretation, then, of what Jesus' perfection amounts to in Hebrews must necessarily address the role that suffering and death play in the perfecting of Jesus.

Peterson's insight that there exists for the author of Hebrews an experiential, vocational dimension to Jesus' perfection is supported by passages like Hebrews 5:7-10:

> In the days of his flesh, Jesus offered up prayers and supplications, with loud cries and tears, to the one who was able to save him from death, and he was heard because of his reverent submission. Although he was a Son, he learned obedience through what he suffered; and having been made perfect [*teleiōtheis*], he became the source of eternal salvation for all who obey him, having been designated by God a high priest according to the order of Melchizedek.

Significantly, the author associates Jesus' perfection in this passage not with the event of the Son's exaltation, but with the quality of obedience that the Son is said to have learned through the painful experience of suffering. Indeed, the reference to the theme of the testing of Jesus only serves to underscore more fully the obedience

---

[43] David Peterson, *Hebrews and Perfection: An Examination of the Concept of Perfection in the Epistle to the Hebrews*, SNTSMS 47 (Cambridge: Cambridge University Press, 1982), 73.

[44] Peterson, *Perfection*, 68.

[45] Johnson, *Hebrews*, 151.

that the author maintains Jesus learned through the experience of suffering (5:8). We noted in the previous chapter that in the ancient world the ideal of education was frequently linked with the notion of discomfort. Particularly in the Greco-Roman philosophical tradition one encounters the idea that God tests the authentic philosopher with painful and challenging circumstances.[46] It is possible that something of this conceptual background may be influencing Hebrews's portrait of Jesus in this passage. It is just as likely, however, that the memory of the passion of Jesus is the primary background for our author's comments concerning the educative suffering that Jesus endured. While the portrait of an anguished Jesus in prayer in 5:7-10 bears some resemblance to the New Testament passion accounts (see Mark 14:32-42; Matt 26:36-46), there are enough differences between the latter and Hebrews 5:7-10 to suggest that Hebrews is not simply supplying here a variant of the Gethsemane tradition.[47] Whatever traditions may underlie 5:7-10, a deeply human portrayal of Jesus becomes immediately apparent to the reader. In contrast to ordinary high priests, who offer external gifts and sacrifices (5:1; 8:3-4; 9:12), Jesus offers to God personal prayers and supplications accompanied by intense emotional investment over the prospect of facing his death (5:7). The notice in 5:7 to "the days of his flesh" suggests that Hebrews has in view here the entire period of Jesus' incarnation and not simply the specific moments before his execution.

But what could it mean for Jesus to have demonstrated such personal investment throughout his entire life? For that matter, what could it mean to say that Jesus learned obedience? Hebrews is likely working here—as Paul seems to be as well (see Gal 2:15-16; Phil 2:8)—from a larger theological assumption that takes for granted the response of faithfulness demonstrated by the Son throughout his human career. The following passage from Paul's Letter to the Romans captures the almost cosmic significance that Paul attaches to the fidelity or faithfulness of the human Jesus: "Therefore just as one man's trespass led to condemnation for all,

[46] DeSilva, *The Letter*, 11–12.
[47] Attridge, *Epistle*, 138.

so one man's act of righteousness leads to justification and life for all. For just as by the one man's disobedience the many were made sinners, so by the one man's obedience the many will be made righteous" (Rom 5:18-19). As he does elsewhere (see 1 Cor 15:20-28), Paul contrasts in this passage from Romans two individuals: Adam and Christ. Viewing the scriptural Adam as a kind of corporate figure of origins, Paul sees Adam as the primordial human being who bequeathed to humanity the tragic legacy of sin and death as a consequence of his disobedience.[48] In contrast, Paul sees Jesus as the human being who, unlike Adam, did not strive to be more (Phil 2:6) but instead lived a life of complete devotion toward God and his fellow human beings. For Paul, such a self-sacrificial life directed toward God and other human beings constitutes the essential essence of what obedience amounts to.

When we read in Hebrews, therefore, of the "reverent submission" of Jesus in 5:7, it would seem that our author is saying that Jesus was obedient in the sense that he was completely open to the will of God throughout his entire life. Moreover, Hebrews shows that Jesus' conformity to the divine will entailed human struggle and development, as indicated by the reference to the "loud cries and tears" (5:7) of Jesus. According to the author of Hebrews, therefore, it was such ever deepening conformity to, and alignment with, the divine will that both constituted the heart of Jesus' education into obedience and accounted for the sinlessness of Jesus (4:15; 7:26; 9:14). On this issue, Luke Timothy Johnson makes the point that although the preexistent Son was the "reflection of the divine glory" (1:3), Jesus still needed to grow into the status of sonship throughout his earthly career.[49] The liberation theologian Jon Sobrino offers a similar observation when he states that, Jesus' "faithfulness is also characterized by process, by having to journey in history."[50]

---

[48] This does not imply, however, that Paul advocates anything like the concept of original sin as described by such figures as St. Augustine.

[49] Johnson, *Hebrews*, 151.

[50] Jon Sobrino, *Christ the Liberator: A View from the Victims*, trans. Paul Burns (Maryknoll, NY: Orbis, 2001), 136.

The repeated references found in Hebrews to the theme of the sinlessness of Jesus (4:15; 7:26) likely refer, therefore, to our author's conviction concerning the experiential struggle of Jesus to live a life of fidelity or faithfulness before God. Jesus is indeed perfected when he is exalted into the heavenly presence of God where, according to our author, the Son now abides forever. However, the author also understands Jesus as having been perfected in the sense that Jesus' response of faithfulness before God matures into, and brings to realization, the faithfulness that God desires in every human being (see 10:36; 13:21). As a reward for the faithfulness which Adam failed to display, but Jesus did display through both his devotion to God's will and life of sacrificial service to others, God exalted the crucified Jesus into heaven. When viewed with these observations in mind, the event of the exaltation of Jesus becomes an integral dimension—but only one dimension—of a more inclusive process of perfection that begins in the incarnation, extends through Jesus' earthly existence and death, and culminates in the heavenly glorification of the preexistent and human Son (9:11-12).

The foregoing analysis that has focused on the representative status and the faithful response of Jesus convincingly demonstrates in my judgment that the author of Hebrews indeed works from a larger theological narrative or story. Although from the perspective of considerations of genre Hebrews is most certainly a letter and not a narrative like the four canonical gospels, it appears legitimate nonetheless to argue that a definite narrative substructure lies at the basis of this letter.[51] Thus, we have seen that, in the grand story that Hebrews narrates, God has a definite intention in creating human beings. The vision of human sover-

---

[51] Abson Prédestin Joseph makes the following observation in reference to 1 Peter: "Although it is true that letters are primarily non-narrative texts, it is also true that letters may and often do contain a narrative substructure wherein events and materials that are essentially narrative in nature are alluded to and become pertinent to understanding the message conveyed in the letter." Abson Prédestin Joseph, *A Narratological Reading of 1 Peter*, Library of New Testament Studies 440 (London: T & T Clark, 2012), 34. In my opinion this statement applies equally well to the Letter to the Hebrews.

eignty expressed in Psalm 8 hints at this intention, but it is just that: a hint. For our author, the true meaning of Psalm 8 becomes apparent only when it is viewed against the cosmic significance of the events of the death and exaltation of Jesus. The entry of the exalted Jesus into the heavenly realm as a consequence of suffering and humiliation reveals that the crowning with glory and honor spoken of in Psalm 8 refers not to earthly sovereignty but to heavenly glory understood as an encounter with God's presence.

Heavenly glory conceived as abiding in God's presence is the destiny of humanity according to Hebrews; more specifically, it is the destiny for the suffering faithful who are addressed in this sermon, a destiny that implies nothing less than communion with God: "But you have come to Mount Zion and to the city of the living God, the heavenly Jerusalem, and to innumerable angels in festal gathering, and to the assembly of the firstborn who are enrolled in heaven" (12:22-23). If such is the vision of the destiny of humankind, it follows that, in the particular narrative substructure exhibited by Hebrews, the author depicts Jesus as the Son who fulfills the divine intention of leading the many sons and daughters of God to glory (2:10) by means of his own personal response of faithful obedience (5:8). Integral, moreover, to this theological narrative is the insistence that Jesus' response of fidelity before God is paradigmatic for the entire community, which is why Jesus is described by the author in 12:2 as the "pioneer and perfecter of our faith."

Chapter 3

The Perfection of the Faithful: On the Path to Glory

I have maintained that an essential aspect of the portrait of Jesus as perfected high priest in Hebrews involves the author's understanding that Jesus progressed in his own personal journey to perfectly embody God's will. Although the author assumes that the Son was preexistent (1:2-3), even divine in some sense (1:8), he also clearly depicts the human Jesus as struggling to live a life in complete conformity to God's will (5:7-8; 10:7).[1] Because Jesus disregarded the shame attached to the cross (12:2), the Son now lives forever as an eternal high priest in the heavenly sanctuary where he forever intervenes on behalf of the faithful (7:25). Integral, therefore, to the spirituality of Hebrews is the author's conviction that the perfect expression of faithfulness on the part of Jesus (3:2; 4:15) led to the transformation of his death into everlasting life in the presence of God (9:24). When the author refers, therefore, to the sinless character of Jesus (4:15; 7:26), he means to indicate to his audience the complete obedience that Jesus demonstrated before God in the context of his earthly ministry (1:9; 5:8; 10:5-9). For the author of Hebrews it was the faithful manner of Jesus' life—no less than the Son's exaltation after death—that enabled Christ to become the "source of eternal salvation" (5:9).

---

[1] Few texts from the New Testament depict Jesus in *unambiguously* divine terms, and the texts that do so tend to conceive of the divine status of Jesus in functional, as opposed to ontological, terms. Jesus is divine, in other words, in the sense that the Son reveals God or makes God present.

For this reason, the paradigmatic role that Jesus plays in Hebrews is not incidental to the spirituality of the letter. In the Son's role as "pioneer" *archēgon* (2:10; 12:2), "forerunner" *prodromos* (6:20), and "perfecter" *teleiōtēn* (12:2) of the faith, Jesus models for the community a path to communion with God that is the joyful destiny for all God's children (2:10). As a consequence of his own response of fidelity before God, Jesus has already achieved this state of joy according to the author of Hebrews (10:12; 12:2). For the faithful who look to Jesus as their pioneer and forerunner, the joy of communion with God constitutes the transcendent hope and goal of their present journey.

The author of Hebrews would undoubtedly have agreed with the definition of spirituality espoused by Gustavo Gutiérrez, who, as we have seen, employs the metaphor of walking or following to capture the essence of what is signified by the concept of the spiritual life. Indeed, throughout Hebrews the theme of movement in general is a pervasive one; and perhaps the most basic movement of all relates to the movement associated with God. Hence, it is God who leads (*eisagagē*) Jesus, described as the "great shepherd of the sheep" (13:20), into the heavenly world where the angels now adore the exalted Son (1:6); and it is God who, through the agency of the Son, is pictured as leading (*agagonta*) the many children to glory (2:10). The author's most evocative use of the terminology of movement, however, is reserved for both the person of Jesus and the socially marginalized faithful whom the Son represents. To this end, Hebrews portrays Jesus as the exalted Son who has "entered" (*eisēlthen*) behind the curtain that shields the holy of holies (6:20); Jesus is the Son who has passed through (*dielēluthota*) the lower heavens (4:14) into heaven itself (9:24); Jesus has entered (*eisēlthen*) a heavenly sanctuary (9:12, 24) as opposed to a humanly constructed sanctuary (8:2; 9:24). The faithful, for their part, "approach" (*proserchestai*) God (4:16; 7:25; 10:1, 22; 11:6; 12:18, 22);[2] and through the response of hope they "draw near"

---

[2] The distinction between the Son who has entered into God's presence and the faithful who approach God is brought out well by John Scholer. See Scholer, *Proleptic Priests*, 197–201.

(*eggizomen*) to God (7:19). The author can even conceive of hope as an existential power that in some way "enters" (*eiserchomenēn*) behind the curtain where the presence of God dwells (6:19). References such as these to the existential experience of salvation presently enjoyed by the audience will more fully occupy our attention near the conclusion of this chapter. There we will examine the specific role that prayer plays in the spirituality of the letter.

Although the author employs the theme of movement for the purpose of encouraging his audience to identify with Jesus as their pioneer and forerunner, at the same time he is careful to underscore significant differences that exist between the experience of the believer and the experience of Jesus. For example, in contrast to Jesus who has attained the goal of a face to face encounter with God (9:24), the faithful this side of the age to come encounter God in a far less direct manner: through the response of hope and prayer (6:18-19; 7:19; 9:14; 13:15).[3] Whereas Jesus now sits at the right hand of God (10:12), the faithful are summoned by the author to continue to run "the race that is set before us" (12:2). For Jesus the journey to the destination of glory has reached its definitive conclusion, but for the faithful the journey is still ongoing. Given the ubiquity of the theme of movement in Hebrews, it is not surprising that many commentators have noted the applicability of the theme of pilgrimage for understanding the broader theological vision of this sermon.[4] Hence, the author encourages the audience to view themselves in company with the biblical patriarchs and matriarchs as sojourners on the earth who look ahead to the heavenly city that has been prepared for them by God (11:16).

Although the community addressed by Hebrews is pictured as not having yet arrived at their heavenly destiny, the author will nonetheless frequently remind them of the benefits of salvation

[3] See Darrell Pursiful, *The Cultic Motif in the Spirituality of the Book of Hebrews* (Lewiston, NY: Edwin Mellen, 1993), 158–59.

[4] See, for example, Ernst Käsemann, *The Wandering People of God: An Investigation of the Letter to the Hebrews*, trans. Roy A. Harrisville and Irving L. Sandberg (Minneapolis: Augsburg, 1984); William G. Johnsson, "The Pilgrimage Motif in the Book of Hebrews," *JBL* 97 (1978): 239–51; deSilva, *The Letter*, 114.

that even now they presently enjoy. The faithful can, for example, look back on the tangible gifts and expressions of the Holy Spirit that attended their conversion experience (2:4; 6:4). In the midst of a Greco-Roman culture in which many viewed death as engendering a permanent closure,[5] the faithful experience, by contrast, an empowering awareness of liberation from the fear of death (2:15). Likewise, the faithful experience in Jesus not simply an eternal high priest but a high priest who empathizes with their struggles (4:25; 2:18) and intercedes with God on their behalf (9:25). Above all the community lives with the confident awareness that their sins have been forgiven by virtue of the death and exaltation of Jesus (1:3; 4:16; 7:25; 9:13-14, 26; 10:19-22).

At the same time, it is clear that Hebrews most characteristically conceives of salvation as a future state. For this reason the author designates his listeners as "those who are to inherit salvation" (1:14); they are a community that looks forward to a world that is to come (2:5); the author encourages them to cultivate their fellowship, since they "see the day approaching" (10:25); theirs is a fellowship defined by the shared experience of "looking for the city that is to come" (13:14); indeed, here they "have no lasting city" (13:14); God's kingdom will ultimately arrive only when all that is created is removed (12:27-28).[6] At present, the most the world has to offer the beleaguered recipients of this sermon is the opportunity to experience the same kind of abuse once experienced by Jesus: "Let us then go to him outside the camp and bear the abuse that he endured. For here we have no lasting city, but we are looking for the city that is to come" (13:13-14).

---

[5] Although ancient notions of the afterlife were quite complex, Paul's summons to the Thessalonian Christians not to "grieve as others do who have no hope" (1 Thess 4:13), suggests a highly pessimistic view of the afterlife for at least some of Paul's auditors.

[6] Hebrews apparently envisions the age to come not as a renewal or transformation of the cosmos (see Rev 21) but instead as the fullness of time when the created realm will be replaced by the eternal, heavenly realm that has always existed. See also Schenck, *Cosmology*, 128–29; David deSilva, "Entering God's Rest: Eschatology and the Socio-Rhetorical Strategy of Hebrews," in *TJ* 21 (2000): 29.

The Example of the Wilderness Generation

Given the emphasis that Hebrews assigns to the futurity of the heavenly destiny awaiting the faithful of God, it should not surprise us that in 3:7–4:13 the author invites his audience to interpret their own heavenly calling (3:1) and companionship with Christ (3:14) in light of the scriptural narrative of the wandering of the people of Israel, who themselves embarked on a journey to cultivate a relationship with God. In an attempt to provide the reader with what I hope will serve as helpful conceptual background, I would like to take this opportunity to analyze briefly the role that Scripture plays in the overall argument of Hebrews. Even first-time readers of Hebrews cannot fail to recognize that the author imparts theological reflection to his audience largely through the creative interpretation of a variety of scriptural texts. We have already noted that the author will sometimes quote scriptural passages as if one hears in them the voice of God, the Spirit, or even Jesus speaking. In such instances scriptural citation becomes synonymous with direct divine speech.[7] Thus in 1:5 the author quotes Psalm 2:7 as the direct speech of God: "For to which of the angels did God ever say, 'You are my Son; today I have begotten you'?" (1:5). And in 3:7-8 the author quotes a section of Psalm 95:7-8 as the words of the Spirit: "Therefore, as the Holy Spirit says, 'Today if you hear his voice, do not harden your hearts as in the rebellion, as on the day of testing in the wilderness" (3:7-8). Jesus is portrayed as the speaker of Isaiah 8:17: "And again, 'I will put my trust in him.' And again, 'Here am I and the children whom God has given me' " (2:13). In contrast to those places in the letter where the author resorts to direct citation of scriptural texts, the author more customarily summarizes scriptural passages that are more narrative in nature, as he does, for example, when he introduces his audience to the mysterious figure of Melchizedek in chapter 7 or when he describes the sacred contents contained within the desert sanctuary (9:1-5).[8] Sometimes both direct citation

---

[7] Pamela M. Eisenbaum, *The Jewish Heroes of Christian History: Hebrews 11 in Literary Context*, SBLDS 156 (Atlanta: Scholars Press, 1997), 92–93.

[8] Ibid., 104.

and summary appear together, as they do in the following passage where the author reflects on the significance of God pledging an oath to Jesus in the context of Psalm 110:4: "This was confirmed with an oath; for others who became priests took their office without an oath, but this one became a priest with an oath, because of the one who said to him, 'The Lord has sworn and will not change his mind, "You are a priest forever" ' " (7:20-21).

In light of these observations, it is clear that the author of Hebrews is not what we might call an impartial interpreter of Scripture. In a manner similar to the scriptural interpretation we encounter in other early Christian texts, the author unabashedly interprets the deeper meaning of Scripture as relating either to particular dimensions of the Christ event or to transcendent heavenly realities. Hence, for our author Psalm 110 no longer refers to the glory of the Davidic monarch, as it did originally, but to Christ's exaltation and priestly vindication (1:13; 5:6; 7:17, 21). Similarly, according to our author the earthly sanctuary that accompanied the ancient Israelites is merely the shadow of the true heavenly sanctuary that Jesus entered upon his exaltation and presently ministers in as heavenly high priest (8:1-2; 9:24). Craig Koester summarizes well the overall scriptural hermeneutic that animates Hebrews when he states that for our author, "the exalted Christ is like a person who stands in the brightness of the sun and casts a shadow upon the earth, so that those who look at the shadow can discern in it the contours of the one who made it. In a similar way, the shadows of the exalted Christ fall on the pages of the OT, allowing the reader to discern in them something of the shape of Christ himself."[9]

As important as it is to appreciate the deeply christological focus of Hebrews's appropriation of Scripture, it is just as crucial to take notice of the author's understanding of the role that Scripture plays in the lives of his audience. The author assumes—and actively encourages his audience to believe—that Scripture provides them with the narrative that puts their own experiences into proper perspective. We have already remarked on some of the

---

[9] Koester, *Hebrews*, 117.

textual evidence of Hebrews, which suggests that the community addressed by our author struggled with the effects of what might sociologically be described as a liminal existence characterized by persecution and marginalization. One way in which the author treats Scripture, therefore, is to draw it into his overall program of providing comfort and hope to a community experiencing the pain of social dislocation. The exordium of Hebrews provides a good illustration of this strategy. It is surely not by accident that Hebrews opens with a highly celebratory portrait of Jesus as the Son of God who is enthroned above the angels (1:4). Indeed, honorific language informs much of the content of the formal introduction to Hebrews (1:1-2:4). Hence, the Son is described as the "heir of all things," and the one through whom God created the cosmos (1:2). Moreover, the Son's position in the heavenly regions is the most honorable of all—seated "at the right hand of the Majesty on high" (1:3). It is crucial to see that scriptural quotation plays more than an accompanying role as part of the author's overall rhetorical task of celebrating the cosmic exaltation of Jesus. By making God the speaker of numerous passages of Scripture that comprise the first half of the exordium (1:5-9), the author enables his audience to imaginatively witness in their mind's eye that moment when the crucifixion of Jesus was overcome by the bestowing of eternal life on Jesus: "And again, when he brings the firstborn into the world, he says, 'Let all God's angels worship him'" (1:6). Somewhat later in the exordium we read: "But of the Son he says, 'Your throne, O God, is forever and ever, and the righteous scepter is the scepter of your kingdom. You have loved righteousness and hated wickedness; therefore God, your God, has anointed you with the oil of gladness beyond your companions'" (1:8-9). It is useful to recall here that the one receiving such honor and vindication is none other than someone who was violently executed in a particularly humiliating and degrading fashion. Crucifixion was a highly public form of execution; and one of its purposes was literally to strip away all vestiges of honor and dignity from the condemned victim. For those in the community who may have been tempted to renounce their confessional ties to such an apparently disgraced person, hearing in these words of Scripture God's honoring of Jesus could potentially provide them with the strength to hold fast to their countercultural commitment. Not only the voice of God but also the exalted nature of God's declaration confirm the honor and glory that the Son now shares in the heavenly realm: "but we do see Jesus, who for a little while was made lower than the angels, now crowned with glory and honor because of the suffering of death" (2:9).

The example above thus shows how the author employs Scripture to give hope to his audience. But it is just as important to see that the author could also quote and paraphrase Scripture in order to warn the community about the prospect of God's judgment. Some of these warnings are quite graphic, as in that instance when the author warns the audience that the price of drawing back from their commitment to Jesus would be to risk to "fall into the hands of the living God" (10:31). This way of appropriating Scripture complements those other sections of the letter where the author warns the community about the risk of neglecting or, even worse, repudiating their present status as beneficiaries of God's grace (see 2:1-3; 4:1; 4:12-13; 10:29; 12:15-17). In addition to their functioning as a way to encourage the audience to show gratitude to God as their benevolent patron,[10] such warning passages function more generally to shape or form the identity of the audience of Hebrews. If we return now to the account of Israel's wandering in the wilderness in 3:7–4:13, we see the author engaging in precisely this kind of identity formation as he attempts to form his audience into a people characterized by the response of faith as opposed to the response of disobedience.

The account of the Exodus of Israel, of which the account of the wilderness wandering is a part, provides our author with a narrative rich with respect to contemporary actualization for the audience of Hebrews. The author would have the community see that, in company with the Exodus generation, they too have experienced liberation, but, in their case, the liberation that has taken place is on a far more impressive scale. For in contrast to the ancient Israelites who were liberated from physical slavery, the likewise marginalized and persecuted community addressed by Hebrews (13:22) had experienced liberation from the slavery of

[10] DeSilva, *The Letter*, 105.

the fear of death (2:15). And just as God had taken hold of the seed of Abraham (2:16) to lead the ancient Israelites out of Egypt through Moses (3:16; 8:9), so, too, had God drawn near to the socially maligned recipients of this sermon by sending the Son to share their humanity (2:14). Above all, just as the faithfulness of Moses led to rest—at least for some—in the form of entrance into the land of Canaan, so too the faithfulness of Jesus has opened the possibility of entrance into what the author describes as the very sabbatical rest of God (4:9-10). Since the community addressed by Hebrews was in danger of repudiating their religious commitment due to the painful experience of social marginalization, the author devotes significant attention in 3:7–4:13 to the terrible consequences that accompanied the lack of fidelity (3:12, 19; 4:11) on the part of the wilderness generation (4:17-19). Aware of the real danger of flagging commitment among his listeners, the author repeatedly warns the community (3:12; 4:1) not to emulate the similar pattern of disobedience that characterized the wilderness generation: "Take care, brothers and sisters, that none of you may have an evil, unbelieving heart that turns away from the living God" (3:12). Similarly, one reads in 4:11: "Let us therefore make every effort to enter that rest, so that no one may fail through such disobedience as theirs." As if to further emphasize such warnings, this section of the sermon concludes in 4:12-13 with the forbidding portrait of a God whose supernatural vision penetrates to the very depths of the human soul.

The author begins this section of Hebrews comprised by 3:1–4:13 by comparing the responses of fidelity demonstrated by both Jesus and Moses, respectively. Moreover, the author depicts both the faithful Moses and the faithful Jesus as presiding over God's house, a metaphor that is likely illustrative of the idea of the people of God (3:1-6):[11]

> Therefore, brothers and sisters, holy partners in a heavenly calling, consider that Jesus, the apostle and high priest of our confession, was faithful to the one who appointed him, just as

[11] See Mitchell, *Hebrews*, 74; Koester, *Hebrews*, 244.

Moses also "was faithful in all God's house." Yet Jesus is worthy
of more glory than Moses, just as the builder of a house has
more honor than the house itself. (For every house is built by
someone, but the builder of all things is God.) Now Moses was
faithful in all God's house as a servant, to testify to the things
that would be spoken later. Christ, however, was faithful over
God's house as a son, and we are his house if we hold firm the
confidence and the pride that belong to hope.

The author's guiding assumption is that Moses and Jesus both
demonstrated faithfulness to the same God who appointed them
for their respective tasks of liberation. While it is obvious that
Hebrews emphasizes the superiority of the Son over Moses, it is
important to see that the author's comparison of the two figures
is not intended to denigrate Moses in any way. Rather, the comparison reveals the author's indebtedness to a principal tenet of
Greco-Roman rhetoric called amplification. Craig Koester observes: "Favorable comparison of a person with someone of high
repute was called amplification (*auxēsis*), which was 'one of the
forms of praise.'"[12] In other words, it is precisely the memory of
the praiseworthy faithfulness of God's greatest servant, Moses
(Num 12:7), that places Jesus' own response of faithfulness into
proper focus for our author.[13] Given the high stature in which
Moses was regarded among Jews in antiquity, there really would
have been no greater intermediary figure with whom to compare
Jesus. Moses was remembered as sharing a close relationship with
God; so close in fact that Moses could even be thought of as having seen God in some sense (see Exod 24:15-18).

According to the author, Moses demonstrated his fidelity before
God by fulfilling the divine commission to lead the people of Israel

---

[12] Koester, *Hebrews*, 248, quoting Aristotle, Rhetoric 19.39. That a diminution of the
stature of Moses is far from our author's thinking is shown by the fact that Moses
will make an appearance later in the letter where he appears as one of the supreme
models of the quality of endurance that defines faith (12:23-28).

[13] See Susan E. Docherty, *The Use of the Old Testament in Hebrews: A Case Study in
Early Jewish Bible Interpretation*, WUNT 2, no. 260 (Tübingen: Mohr Siebeck, 2009),
184.

out from their slavery in Egypt (3:16). The faithfulness demonstrated by Jesus is best seen by paying careful attention to the
hallmarks of the Christology articulated in Hebrews 2:10-18. Like
Moses, Jesus was also appointed for a task, but his task was to
bring humanity to glory (2:10); a task brought to realization, para-
doxically, through the incarnation, faithful death, and subsequent
exaltation of the Son. I have already highlighted the connection
that the author of Hebrews makes between the idea of the perfection of Jesus and the exaltation of the Son—namely, that Jesus is
perfected or brought to completion in the sense of entering into
the heavenly sanctuary where the presence of God dwells. I have
moreover stated that the author conceives of this destiny of glory
also as the reward for the faithful who endure persecution. The
essential reason, therefore, why the author can affirm in 3:3 that
Jesus is deserving of greater glory than Moses is because he understands the liberation brought by the Son to be qualitatively superior:
it is nothing less than the liberation of a heavenly destiny (3:1)
conceived of metaphorically as "rest" (3:11, 18; 4:1, 3, 5, 10).

This theme of the heavenly destiny of rest for God's faithful that
has been made possible by the obedient death and heavenly exaltation of Jesus underlies the evocative metaphor of a house employed in 3:2-6. In these verses the author pointedly affirms that
the recipients of his sermon—including himself—constitute
Christ's house. The metaphor of a house is noteworthy, in the first
instance, for its evident pastoral power, since it implies that the
divine household is comprised of precisely these socially beleaguered Christians, who have experienced the loss of their earthly
possessions in conjunction with their honorable standing in the
surrounding culture (10:33-34). Indeed, the power of this particular metaphor owes much to its implicit social implications.
Aware of the higher honor that would have been accorded to
natural-born sons in an ancient household, the audience would
quite naturally grant that due to his status as a Son, Jesus would
have greater honor than Moses who is described as a servant. At
the same time, the metaphor of the household also contains pro-
found theological implications. Functioning as a spatial, as well
as a social reality, the metaphor effectively foreshadows the references that will occur later in the letter to the heavenly sanctuary

first entered by Jesus. By designating his listeners both as "partners of a heavenly calling" (3:1) and "partners with Christ" (3:14), the author endeavors to assure his audience that they are destined, in company with Jesus, to have their future dwelling place in the heavenly sanctuary, provided that they do not fall away from the living God through unbelief (3:12).

The author recites next the paradigmatic disobedience of the wilderness generation by selectively quoting in Hebrews 3:7-11 a portion of Psalm 95:7-11:

> Therefore, as the Holy Spirit says, "Today, if you hear his voice, do not harden your hearts as in the rebellion, as on the day of testing in the wilderness, where your ancestors put me to the test, though they had seen my works for forty years. Therefore I was angry with that generation, and I said, 'They always go astray in their hearts, and they have not known my ways.' As in my anger I swore, 'They will not enter my rest.'"

Despite the calamitous warning that characterizes this portion of the psalm, it is important to remember that the prevailing tone of Psalm 95 is one of celebration. Indeed, much of the psalm consists of the psalmist praising the Lord, the God of Israel, for what the psalmist describes as the Lord's power over the creation as well as the Lord's commitment to the covenant people of Israel: "O come, let us worship and bow down, let us kneel before the LORD, our Maker! For he is our God, and we are the people of his pasture, and the sheep of his hand" (Ps 95:6-7). It is precisely the memory of God's liberation of the covenant people of God—in fulfillment of the commitment made to Abraham—that warrants the admonition in the remainder of the psalm always to trust the future that God has in store for the people.

The events recalled by Psalm 95 refer to two dramatic acts of disobedience on the part of the ancient Israelites that followed the flight from Egypt: the angry plea for water (Exod 17:1-7; Num 20:2-13) and the anxiety that consumed the people in response to the unfavorable report of the spies who were commissioned to reconnoiter the land of Canaan (Num 13:25-14:45). These stories appealed to the author of Hebrews since they complemented in important ways the experiences of societal scorn endured by the community. By way of illustration, note that in Exodus 17:1-7, the complaint of the assembly concerning the lack of water in the wilderness is associated with the attraction the Israelites felt for the comparative security of Egypt: "But the people thirsted there for water; and the people complained against Moses and said, 'Why did you bring us out of Egypt, to kill us and our children and livestock with thirst?'" (Exod 17:3). The keen desire for security on the part of the wilderness generation is described in even more vivid terms in a similar version of the incident narrated in the book of Numbers: "Why have you brought us up out of Egypt, to bring us to this wretched place? It is no place for grain, or figs, or vines, or pomegranates; and there is no water to drink" (Num 20:5). It is quite possible that our author recognizes that a similar desire for comfort and security animates many among the persecuted addressees of his sermon. Faced with the repeated experiences of reproach and scorn by the larger culture (10:32-33; 13:13), the temptation to turn away from God (3:12; 10:39) and seek more conventional grants of honor and acceptance from the wider culture would have proved irresistible for many within the community. This prospect may account for, at least in part, the intriguing description of Moses found in Hebrews 11:24-27:

> By faith Moses, when he was grown up, refused to be called a son of Pharaoh's daughter, choosing rather to share ill-treatment with the people of God than to enjoy the fleeting pleasures of sin. He considered abuse suffered for the Christ to be greater wealth than the treasures of Egypt for he was looking ahead to the reward. By faith he left Egypt, unafraid of the king's anger; for he persevered as though he saw him who is invisible.

The references in this passage to "ill-treatment" and "abuse" are quite likely chosen by the author with the marginal status of his listeners in mind.[14] The figure of Moses functions as a heroic

---

[14] The Greek word for "abuse" that occurs in 11:26 (*oneidismon*) is the same word employed in 10:33 (*oneidismois*) to describe the public abuse suffered by the community in their recent past. In 13:13 the same noun appears in connection with the abuse endured by Jesus.

example of the kind of countercultural behavior that the author of Hebrews desires his audience to aspire to. In company with several other righteous individuals who are celebrated for their faith in chapter 11, Moses embodies for our author a life that sets its sight upon a reward that is more honorable than either earthly approval or societal security: "But as it is, they desire a better country, that is, a heavenly one. Therefore God is not ashamed to be called their God; indeed, he has prepared a city for them" (11:16). Without at all minimizing the painful experience of loss of honor and security that accompanied the conversion experience of many among his addressees, the author desires the community to understand that God does not endorse the verdict of shame lodged against them by the larger culture. With God as their patron, there is no need for the community to turn away in disbelief.[15] Indeed, perhaps the single most important issue that emerges in the scriptural accounts of Israel's disobedience relates precisely to the issue of faithfulness or trust. Significantly, the incident at Massah and Meribah concludes with the following reference to Moses: "He called the place Massah and Meribah, because the Israelites quarreled and tested the LORD, saying, 'Is the LORD among us or not?'" (Exod 17:7). Accompanying the insecurity that was engendered in the hearts of the wilderness generation at the prospect of facing an uncertain future was the more fundamental failure of faith or trust that God was present in their midst. A similar preoccupation with the theme of the abiding presence of God appears in the account of the unfavorable report about Canaan narrated in the book of Numbers. Upon receiving the news that the inhabitants of Canaan appear formidable and unconquerable, the Israelites respond by voicing their collective desire to return to Egypt. In an attempt to avert God's decision to destroy the people over this failure of vision, Moses says the following:

> But Moses said to the LORD, "Then the Egyptians will hear of it, for in your might you brought up this people from among them, and they will tell the inhabitants of this land. They have

---

[15] Insightful reflections on the role of God as patron can be found in deSilva, *The Letter*, 95–138.

heard that you, O LORD, are in the midst of this people; for you O LORD, are seen face to face, and your cloud stands over them and you go in front of them, in a pillar of cloud by day and in a pillar of fire by night. Now if you kill this people all at one time, then the nations who have heard about you will say, 'It is because the Lord was not able to bring this people into the land he swore to give them that he has slaughtered them in the wilderness.' " (Num 14:13-16)

Integral to these accounts is the emphasis placed on the abiding presence of God in the midst of the wilderness generation. As demonstrated by the pillar of cloud by day and the pillar of fire by night, God accompanies the assembly of the Israelites at every step of their journey. The essential disobedience demonstrated by the majority of the wilderness generation, therefore, resides in their failure to trust in that abiding presence. Hence the question at Massah and Meribah: "Is the Lord among us or not?"

Rest as Metaphor for Communion with God and Christ

The author's extensive rehearsal relating to the disobedience of the wilderness generation functions rhetorically to dissuade the listeners of Hebrews from abandoning their countercultural commitment to Jesus (see 10:35). Like the ancient Israelites in the wilderness, the first century auditors of Hebrews also faced the danger of lapsing into disbelief (3:12). According to our author, the consequences of giving way to such disbelief would amount to a falling away "from the living God" (3:12), in addition to a failure to enter into what our author evocatively describes as God's rest (3:11, 18; 4:1, 3, 5, 10, 11). The metaphor of God's "rest" (*katapausis*) constitutes one of the major themes of the entire passage comprised by 3:1–4:13. Suggestive clues into the meaning of this metaphor are foreshadowed at strategic points earlier in the sermon. Already in 1:14, the author refers to a salvation (*sōtērian*) that the community stands to inherit. And in 2:3 the author warns the community concerning the danger of neglecting "so great a salvation." In 2:10 the author carefully links the idea of salvation with the goal of entering into God's glory as a consequence of the perfection or completion of Jesus through the sufferings that he endured. It is not until chapter 3, however, where the author's distinctive concept of salvation as suggestive of both a heavenly destiny (3:1) as well as participation in Christ (3:14) becomes clearer. Complementing other places in the sermon where the author places greater value on heavenly as opposed to earthly realities, the metaphor of rest functions to confront the audience with the prospect of the goal of communion with God within the heavenly sanctuary. For this reason, it would be a mistake to construe the theme of rest in Hebrews as referring to the physical land of Canaan. Instead the author's point is that God's rest signifies not any kind of tangible, physical region at all. This explains why the author will make a point of saying in 4:8 that Joshua had not actually given the people rest. On the face of it the statement is patently false, since Joshua did in fact enter the land of promise, namely, Canaan (Josh 21:43), thereby providing rest for the Israelites. But this is not the rest that our author has in mind. Authentic rest for our author (that is, the rest that is characteristic of the nature of God) refers to the divine realm that the faithful will one day enter, just as their heavenly forerunner Jesus once did.[16]

The way in which our author arrives at this conclusion derives from his skillful use of a Jewish principle of scriptural exegesis whereby a specific scriptural passage is interpreted in light of another passage on the basis of a word or phrase that both passages hold in common.[17] The procedure works in the following manner: Psalm 95 concludes in verse eleven with God swearing an oath that functions to prevent the majority of the Israelites who left Egypt from entering God's rest: the promised land of Canaan. In the Greek translation of this verse derived from the Septuagint,

---

[16] See deSilva, "Entering God's Rest," 39. James Thompson makes the important point that the theme of rest can be thought of in spatial categories, provided that the interpreter conceives of this spatial category as a thoroughly transcendent reality that abides beyond the visible creation. See Thompson, *The Beginnings*, 99.

[17] The technical name of the principle is *gezera shawa*. For a concise definition of the term see Eisenbaum, *The Jewish Heroes*, 95. See also, Randall C. Gleason, "The Old Testament Background of Rest in Hebrews 3:7–4:11" *BSac* 157 (2000): 283.

the word denoting rest is a noun. The author of Hebrews links this Greek noun with the verbal form of rest that appears in the Septuagint version of Genesis 2:2, a passage that envisions God as resting from the labor involved in the creation of the world over the course of six days.[18] By joining the verb for rest found in Genesis 2:2 with the Greek noun for rest found in Psalm 95:11, the author more precisely redefines the rest of God as implying the sabbatical rest of God—namely, that mysterious, almost timeless moment when God rested from the divine labor. The resulting idea is theologically provocative to say the least. To enter God's rest, a rest redefined precisely as God's sabbatical rest (4:9), is to have "a share in God's eternal 'sabbatical' repose."[19] Celebrating the dignity and grandeur of this rest, the author urges the community to make every effort to enter into it. In this transcendent rest they will encounter both the great high priest Jesus who has already passed through the heavens (4:14), as well as the throne of God where the divine presence dwells (4:16).

Entering God's Rest:
The Present Dimension of Salvation

Given that our author's characteristic way of describing salvation is to conceive of it as a future reality, it is interesting to see that in several places in 3:1–4:13 the author employs terminology suggestive of the idea that rest is something the believer can enjoy in the present. In 4:3, for example, the author describes both himself and his audience as those "who have believed enter that rest." Similarly, in 4:11 the author urges his listeners to "make every effort to enter that rest." Some of the complexity involved in this issue relates in part to the ambiguity of Greek grammar. In both 4:3 and 4:11 the verb meaning "to enter" occurs in the present tense. The present tense in Greek allows some flexibility in terms of English translation. Specifically, the Greek present tense can some-

---

[18] The latter passage provided a theological justification for the mandated day of rest, namely, the Sabbath.

[19] Harold W. Attridge, "Let Us Strive to Enter That Rest: The Logic of Hebrews 4:1-11," *HTR* 73 (1980): 283.

times be used to denote the idea of progressive or ongoing movement in the present.[20] If our author is employing the present tense in this sense in both 4:3 and 4:11, then his intention may be to suggest that his listeners find themselves on the cusp of entering God's rest. They find themselves, in other words, on the way. Full or complete entry into God's rest this side of the age to come is impossible. What is possible for the people of God is to begin a journey that will continually be in process until the arrival of Jesus (9:28) and the inauguration of the eternally abiding Kingdom of God (12:28).[21] In commenting on these passages, deSilva makes the important observation that the essential manner in which the community takes steps in their continual journey of striving to enter into God's rest is to resist succumbing to the painful effects of social marginalization at the hands of the dominant Greco-Roman culture.[22] On this reading, the community's collective striving to enter into God's rest relates in meaningful ways to their ongoing project of cultivating and redoubling their commitment to Jesus. While I find myself in agreement with deSilva that a vital sociological dimension is at work here, I also think that the journey into God's rest envisioned by the author likely implies more than just such a redoubling of commitment to Jesus in the face of societal scorn. The author's ultimate concern is, at heart, theological in nature. More specifically, I propose that in the thinking of our author it is the liturgical life of the community and, in particular, the experience of prayer, that serves as the primary vehicle for experiencing, on this side of the age to come, God's presence conceived metaphorically as rest.

The Present Dimension of Salvation: The Cleansing of Conscience

Jesus is not the only figure in Hebrews who is said to have experienced perfection. There are three instances in the letter where

[20] DeSilva, "Entering God's Rest," 30–32. The formal term is that of an ingressive present. See Mitchell, *Hebrews*, 97.

[21] DeSilva, "Entering God's Rest," 31.

[22] Ibid., 32.

the author reflects directly on what perfection means for the life of the faithful (9:9; 10:1, 14). As we have already noted, in the broadest sense believers experience perfection in the age to come when they inherit a kingdom that transcends all manner of creaturely existence (12:26-27; 13:14) and enter fully into the glory of God's transcendent presence. Perfection for the faithful refers ultimately, then, to the completion of the divine plan of salvation when God will endow humanity with honor and glory (2:5-10).[23] As experienced in the lives of the faithful, however, perfection also has a present dimension according to the author of Hebrews, since those who participate in Christ (3:1, 6) are pictured by the author as already enjoying access to God in their earthly existence (4:16; 6:19; 7:19; 10:19-22; 12:22-24).[24] In order to demonstrate how this understanding informs our author's thinking I first need to address the profoundly sacrificial appraisal of the Christ event that we encounter in Hebrews.

Integral to the author's understanding of Jesus as a perfect high priest is his conviction that the death of Jesus constitutes a sacrificial offering for sin: "But when Christ had offered for all time a single sacrifice for sins, 'he sat down at the right hand of God'" (10:12). This sacrificial theme is announced initially in the exordium of the letter (1:3), before being developed more fully in the middle section of Hebrews, particularly in chapters 9 and 10 (see 7:27; 9:14, 26, 28; 10:10). The author's precise conception, however, of how the sacrificial offering of Jesus atones for sin is complex. On the one hand, certain passages in the letter seem to presuppose the traditional appraisal of Jesus' death on the cross as an expiatory sacrifice that purifies (1:3; 9:14) or cleanses away sin. For example, after describing briefly the activity of the human high priest in the context of the Day of Atonement ritual (9:6-7), the author makes a point of contrasting the Levitical rite with the activity of Jesus: "But when Christ came as a high priest of the good things that have come, then through the greater and perfect tent (not made with hands, that is, not of this creation), he entered once for all

[23] Lindars, *Theology*, 44.
[24] Scholer, *Proleptic*, 199.

into the Holy Place, not with the blood of goats and calves, but with his own blood, thus obtaining eternal redemption" (9:11-12). Similarly, the author makes a direct link in 10:5-10 between Jesus' earthly ministry that culminated in his death and the resulting sanctification that followed upon the commitment of Jesus to put the will of God into effect. It would seem that in both of these passages the author works with a model of atonement that is quite similar to the way Paul describes the death of Jesus in Romans 3:25 as "a sacrifice of atonement by his blood."

In other passages, however, the author can speak of the high priestly offering of Jesus in a manner that suggests that purification from sin takes place in heaven as a result of the exaltation of Jesus to eternal life in God's presence: "For Christ did not enter a sanctuary made by human hands, a mere copy of the true one, but he entered into heaven itself, now to appear before the presence of God on our behalf. Nor was it to offer himself again and again, as the high priest enters the Holy Place with blood that is not his own" (9:24-25).[25] It is possible that the author may not have been completely clear himself as to the precise moment when atonement, or for that matter, when Jesus became a high priest, took place.[26] We must reckon with the fact that the author's theological reflections are not as systematic as we might like them to be. What does appear to be clear, however, is that the death/exaltation of Jesus, when appropriated by faith, accomplishes not just the forgiveness of sin, but strikingly the very removal of sin according to the author: "But as it is, he has appeared once for all at the age to remove sin by the sacrifice of himself" (9:26). In the conceptual universe of the author, sin appears as a barrier that separates people from God, and, with the removal of sin, authentic access to God becomes a present reality for the faithful:

> Therefore, my friends, since we have confidence to enter the sanctuary by the blood of Jesus, by the new and living way that he opened for us through the curtain (that is, through his flesh), and since we have a great priest over the house of God, let us

[25] See David Moffitt, "Unveiling Jesus' Flesh," 71–84.
[26] Koester, *Hebrews*, 110.

> approach with a true heart in full assurance of faith, with our
> hearts sprinkled clean from an evil conscience and our bodies
> washed with pure water. (10:19-22)

Earlier in the letter the author described the entrance of the Son
into the heavenly sanctuary that is superior to any transient sanctuary on earth (9:24). And within that sanctuary Jesus is said to
have appeared before the presence of God (9:24). The somewhat
misleading translation "to enter," which is found in the NRSV, is
a translation of a single Greek noun, *eisodon*, which means literally
a "door" or "portal." Strikingly, the author of Hebrews encourages
the believer to proceed through the portal opened through Jesus'
death to encounter God on the other side. Here I propose that
Hebrews is concerned to place before the community the present
dimension of salvation that stems from Christ's own deeply personal act of faithfulness (9:14; 10:9). Hence, the experiential dimension that characterized Jesus' own perfection through his living
out of God's will (5:7-9) engenders within the lives of believers
the experiential "confidence" (*parrēsian*) of communion with God
in the present (4:16). For the author of Hebrews, it is this lived
experience of direct access to God that constitutes what perfection
means for the believer this side of the age to come.

The same weight given to the experiential dimension of salvation appears also in the frequent references in the letter to the
purification of the conscience (*suneidēsin*) of the faithful (9:9, 14;
10:2, 22). Hence the author writes:

> This is a symbol of the present time, during which gifts and
> sacrifices are offered that cannot perfect the conscience
> [*suneidēsin*] of the worshipper. . . . For if the blood of goats
> and bulls, with the sprinkling of the ashes of a heifer, sanctifies
> those who have been defiled so that their flesh is purified, how
> much more will the blood of Christ, who through the eternal
> Spirit offered himself without blemish to God, purify our con-
> science [*suneidēsin*] from dead works to worship the living God!
> (9:9-14)

The term "conscience," which appears frequently in the letters of
Paul, conveys the basic idea of awareness and frequently suggests

the nuance of moral awareness.[27] Hebrews employs the term to draw attention to that which is most inward within a human being. For the believer the sacrificial death of the Son engenders the experiential conviction of purification, by which our author means the act of expiation or the cleansing of sin.[28] Such cleansing reaches far into the depths of the personality in the sense that even the consciousness of sin is understood to be removed (10:2). Since the author of Hebrews perceives sin to be an obstacle that separates God from human beings, the purification of the conscience that the sacrificial death of Jesus accomplishes enables the believer to draw inwardly near to the transcendent presence of God. The author connects this notion of internal cleansing of the conscience with the scriptural expectation of God's renewal of the covenant found in Jeremiah 31:31-34: "The days are surely coming, says the Lord, when I will establish a new covenant with the house of Israel and with the house of Judah. . . . This is the covenant that I will make with the house of Israel after those days, says the Lord: I will put my laws in their minds, and write them on their hearts, and I will be their God, and they shall be my people" (8:8-10). The importance that the prophecy from Jeremiah has for the author of Hebrews is borne out by the fact that the author quotes Jeremiah twice (8:8-12; 10:16-17).

The idea of a renewed covenant made possible through the death of Jesus likely appealed to the author since the idea of covenant implies relationship. In 9:18-21 the author recalls the covenant ratification ritual as described in Exodus 24:3-8. Central to the scriptural account is the focus on the commitment of the ancient Israelites to obey the commandments of the Lord and thus become God's holy or sanctified people (Exod 24:3, 7). Put another way, the promise made by the Israelites to live in obedience to the laws of the covenant functions as a way to honor God's loving decision to live in relationship with the Jewish people. Moreover, the commitment of the Israelites to live lives of obedience is pictured as being confirmed through the sacrificial rite of animal sacrifice (Exod 24:5-8). Working with such a communal understanding of

[27] Attridge, *Epistle*, 242.
[28] Ibid., 251–52.

the idea of covenant, the author of Hebrews sees the promise of a renewed and deeper relationship with God fulfilled in the shedding of the blood of Jesus (9:13-14; 10:14).

This understanding of perfection conceived as both direct access to God and renewed relationship with God bears a direct connection to the author's criticism of the cultic activity that took place under what the author characterizes as the first covenant (8:7, 13; 9:1). Although in the central section of the letter Hebrews actually refers to three separate sacrificial rituals, it is clear that the ritual of the Day of Atonement as described in Leviticus 16:1-34 is foremost in the author's mind.[29] The author's treatment of this ritual is, however, highly selective: "Such preparations having been made, the priests go continually into the first tent to carry out their ritual duties; but only the high priest goes into the second, and he but once a year, and not without taking the blood that he offers for himself and for the sins committed unintentionally by the people" (9:6-7). In Hebrews 9:1-5, the author supplies a selective synopsis of the layout of the wilderness sanctuary in accordance with the scriptural account found in Exodus 25–27. While the description of the sanctuary in Hebrews is ambiguous at points, there appears to be a clear motivation on the part of the author to make a distinction between an interior compartment of the sanctuary in contrast to an outer vestibule.[30] With this visualization of the sanctuary in mind, the author depicts in 9:6-7 the movement of the human high priest as he proceeds to pass behind the curtain within the sanctuary. Once behind the curtain, the high priest would proceed to sprinkle the sacrificial blood of both a bull and a goat upon the so-called mercy seat, where it was believed that the presence of God invisibly dwelled (Lev 16:2). The entire ritual was understood to effect the expiation or cleansing away of sin that served as a barrier separating God from the covenant people (Lev 16:11-16).

---

[29] The Day of Atonement ritual in 9:6-7, 25; 10:3-4 (Lev 16:1-19); the Sinai covenant ratification ritual in 9:18-21 (Exod 24:1-8); and the ritual of the red heifer in 9:13 (Num 19:1-13).

[30] Mitchell, *Hebrews*, 178–79.

With the faith commitment already in place that the death and exaltation of Jesus provides expiation for sin, the author of Hebrews interprets the selectively chosen features of the Day of Atonement ritual as indicative of an overall pattern of imperfection hinted at long ago (9:8-9). On the one hand, the very repetition of sacrifices under the first covenant signals imperfection for Hebrews (10:1-3, 11-12), since lasting purification from the consciousness of sin was never achieved (10:2-3). On the other hand, the author links the deeper imperfection of previous sacrificial rites to their failure to secure the goal of gaining access to God. Ultimately, it is this experiential conviction (10:22) of dwelling in the presence of God that is the real issue for the author. Thus, while the author of Hebrews grants that God's presence dwelled within the wilderness sanctuary, at the same time he believes that the divine glory was shielded by a curtain that restricted access to God to all but the high priest; and even he could only enter behind the curtain once a year (9:7, 25). The connections that appear in Hebrews between the concepts of perfection, purification of conscience, and communion with God are nicely brought together in the author's own words:

> Since the law has only a shadow of the good things to come and not the true form of these realities, it can never, by the same sacrifices that are continually offered year after year, make perfect those who approach. Otherwise, would they not have ceased being offered, since the worshippers, cleansed once for all, would no longer have consciousness of sin? But in these sacrifices there is a reminder of sin year after year. For it is impossible for the blood of bulls and goats to take away sins (10:1-4).

The Present Dimension of Salvation: The Role of Prayer in the Spirituality of Hebrews

In their book *Christian Spirituality: Themes from the Tradition*, Cunningham and Egan define the role of prayer in the context of Christian spirituality in the following way:

> The very act or gesture of prayer "says" that an individual or
> a community has a conviction, symbolized by the act or gesture
> of prayer itself, that the person or community recognizes some-
> one with whom they have a deep and meaningful connection
> who is greater than, and concerned about, those who pray. . . .
> In that general sense, then, prayer positively signals commu-
> nication with an Other and, simultaneously, says, in effect, that
> a person is not totally self-sufficient and does not regard himself
> or herself as totally autonomous or alone. Prayer, in other words,
> presupposes some type of relationship.[31]

In their accounts of the public ministry of Jesus, the gospels
frequently emphasize the prayer life of Jesus.[32] Although this emphasis is less pronounced in Hebrews, there is one passage in the
letter that offers a dramatic portrayal of Jesus in prayer: "In the
days of his flesh, Jesus offered up prayers and supplications, with
loud cries and tears, to the one who was able to save him from
death, and he was heard because of his reverent submission" (5:7).
Here Jesus is presented as coming before God with the expectation
that God will hear him and, in fact, Jesus is said to have been heard
by God on account of the reverence or piety that Jesus displays.
Given Hebrews's explicit notice concerning the loud cries and
tears of Jesus, we might reasonably argue that Jesus struggles in
this passage to align his will to a deeper transcendent source that
lies outside himself. Through the act of prayer, in other words,
Jesus cultivates a deeper relationship with the Father, a relationship that is ultimately rewarded with the gift of exaltation to new
life after the events of the passion.

While the depiction of Jesus engaged in prayer is rare in Hebrews, the author frequently offers glimpses into what could be
described as the liturgical life of the community. For example, in
12:28 the author celebrates the unshakeable kingdom that the
community will soon receive by encouraging his audience to "give
thanks, by which we offer to God an acceptable worship with

---

[31] Cunningham and Egan, *Christian Spirituality*, 66–67.
[32] Some examples include Mark 1:35; 14:35, 39; Matt 26:36, 39, 42, 44; Luke 3:21;
6:12.

reverence and awe." And following directly upon the author's exhortation to the community to emulate the suffering that Jesus endured, is the following exhortation: "Through him, then, let us continually offer a sacrifice of praise to God, that is, the fruit of lips that confess his name" (13:15). Perhaps the most significant references to prayer appear, however, in those passages where the community is depicted as drawing near to, or approaching, God. The first of these passages occurs in the conclusion of the summary statement that brings the first major section of the letter to a conclusion: "Let us therefore approach the throne of grace with boldness, so that we may receive mercy and find grace to help in time of need" (4:16). The same emphasis on the theme of approaching God also appears in 7:25, in that section of the letter where the author relates the motif of the superior priesthood of Jesus to the mysterious figure of Melchizedek: "Consequently he is able for all time to save those who approach God through him, since he always lives to make intercession for them." The author similarly links the theme of approaching God with the theme of perfection in 10:1: "Since the law has only a shadow of the good things to come and not the true form of these realities, it can never, by the same sacrifices that are continually offered year after year, make perfect those who approach." Later in this same chapter the author links the approach to God on the part of the faithful with the theme of the cleansed conscience: "Let us approach with a true heart in full assurance of faith, with our hearts sprinkled clean from an evil conscience and our bodies washed with pure water" (10:22).[33] Since we have already noted that entry into heaven is conceived by the author of Hebrews ultimately as a future destiny for the faithful, how are we to interpret these many references in the letter to the faithful approaching God in the present?[34]

It is exegetically significant that in all these passages the author employs the identical Greek verb: *proserchomai*. This verb is frequently used in the Septuagint to denote a particular liturgical

[33] See also 11:6; 12:18, 22.

[34] Scholer puts the matter this way: "The Christians are still on earth suffering the human foibles that accompany worldly existence, so that the[y] can not enter, physically, into the heavenly holy of holies." Scholer, *Proleptic*, 107.

movement, namely, the act of coming before the Lord in prayer.[35] Moreover, the fact that the author makes a correlation between the movement of drawing near to God and the cleansing of the human conscience (10:22) suggests that the author thinks of this approach along the lines of an inward turning to God. Through prayer, in other words, the faithful experience a foretaste of the full communion that they will have with God in the future when they arrive in the heavenly realm at the end of the age. Of the various passages in which the language of approaching God appears, two are especially illustrative of the role that prayer plays in the spirituality of Hebrews. The first is the summary passage that marks the transition to that section of the letter where the author will begin to reflect in more detail on the theme of the high priesthood of Jesus:

> Since, then, we have a great high priest who has passed through the heavens, Jesus, the Son of God, let us hold fast to our confession. For we do not have a high priest who is unable to sympathize with our weaknesses, but we have one who in every way has been tested as we are, yet without sin. Let us therefore approach the throne of grace with boldness, so that we may receive mercy and find grace to help in time of need. (Heb 4:14-16)

The image of the throne of God functions primarily to convey the idea of the royal majesty of God. When combined with the references to God's mercy and grace, the image of the divine throne is illustrative as well of the qualities of beneficence and kindness that were expected character traits of an ideal king or ruler.[36] Moreover, since Jesus is described as the high priestly Son of God who has "passed through the heavens," the throne image underscores the heavenly region where the transcendent presence of God uniquely dwells. We have already noted that the Greek term *proserchomai* is used in certain texts of the Greek translation

---

[35] Ibid., 100.

[36] Koester, *Hebrews*, 284–85; see also Scholer, *Proleptic*, 105.

of the Jewish Bible to denote prayer. Although it is true that the precise Greek word for prayer is not used in the passage from Hebrews quoted above, it is perhaps significant that this transitional passage appears in close proximity to those verses that do specifically envision Jesus engaged in the act of praying.[37] Another potential clue that prayer is in view in 4:11-16 is the reference to God dispensing mercy and help to the faithful. The author characterizes God as the one who could save Jesus from impending suffering and death. Although it is certainly true that God is not pictured as delivering Jesus from his fate, we nonetheless read that God heard Jesus, presumably by raising him from the dead. The pastoral message to the audience of Hebrews seems clear: just as Jesus received divine mercy and help by being exalted to new life on the basis of his fidelity or faithfulness before God, so the persecuted members of the community can also expect God to deliver, provided that they endure, just as Jesus endured.

The second passage where the liturgical life of the community appears to be in view is found in 12:18-24:

> You have not come to something that can be touched, a blazing fire, and darkness, and gloom, and a tempest, and the sound of a trumpet, and a voice whose words made the hearers beg that not another word be spoken to them. (For they could not endure the order that was given, "If even an animal touches the mountain, it shall be stoned to death." Indeed, so terrible was the sight that Moses said, "I tremble with fear.") But you have come to Mount Zion and to the city of the living God, the heavenly Jerusalem, and to innumerable angels in festal gathering, and to the assembly of the firstborn who are enrolled in heaven, and to God the judge of all, and to the spirits of the righteous made perfect, and to Jesus, the mediator of a new covenant, and to the sprinkled blood that speaks a better word than the blood of Abel.

As he did earlier in 3:7–4:13, once more the author recalls for the audience foundational events from the story of the Exodus.

---

[37] Scholer, *Proleptic*, 108.

In this particular instance, the author rehearses for his listeners selective aspects of that scene in the book of Exodus where the Israelites entered the wilderness of Sinai and camped at the base of Mount Sinai (Exod 19:2). It is helpful to examine Hebrews 12:18-24 in light of the Sinai event as a whole as related in Exodus 19–24. The arrival of the Israelites at Mount Sinai is a pivotal event in the Exodus story, since it is at this stage within the narrative that the assembly of the Israelites is pictured as committing themselves to obey the ordinances of the Lord. As a result of this commitment on the part of the people, Moses performs a covenant ratification ritual complete with the sacrificial shedding of blood to formalize the covenant between God and the people. The scriptural story focuses, therefore, on the idea of relationship, namely, the Lord's commitment to be the God of this particular people provided that they obey the Lord's commandments: "Now therefore if you obey my voice and keep my covenant, you shall be my treasured possession out of all the peoples" (Exod 19:5).

It is important to note, however, that the Exodus account is deeply informed by a paradox. In Exodus 19:17, we read that Moses brings the assembly of Israelites out to encounter or to meet God. However, it is only Moses and a select few who actually see the God of Israel (Exod 24:9-11). For the rest of the assembly the encounter with the Lord is fraught with dreadful displays of the power of the Lord's presence compounded by explicit prohibitions warning of the danger of approaching too near to the divine presence within the cloud. Hence the paradox is that while a divine appearance does take place, the theophany is nevertheless deeply foreboding and limited to a privileged few.

The author of Hebrews focuses on the theme of the encounter with the God of Israel as narrated in Exodus 19–24 and attempts to demonstrate to his audience the meaningful contrast that they should perceive between their situation and the experience of the wilderness generation. The key to understanding 12:18-24 centers on the distinction that the author customarily makes elsewhere in the letter concerning the contrast between the earthly and the heavenly. Hence, in 12:18 the author informs the community that they have not approached something that can be touched, while in 12:22 he notes that they have drawn near to the heavenly Jerusalem. The author's notice about the presence of both myriads of angels and the righteous dead functions to provide the audience with a vision ahead of time of what the heavenly region, their ultimate destiny, will look like. Even the reference to God as judge has a heavenly ring to it, given that the theme of the judgment of God implies a throne from which to dispense judgment. As we have already seen, the image of God's throne denotes the theme of the heavenly majesty of God. It is important to emphasize here, however, that the author is not saying that the community has in fact arrived in heaven, or even that they somehow mystically attain perfect union with God while on earth.[38] Nonetheless, the author does appear to envision in this passage a genuine encounter with God that all but guarantees the entrance of the faithful into this joyous realm at the final end of days. The untouchable nature of their heavenly destiny suggests, however, that the heavenly Jerusalem can only be accessed this side of the age to come in a correspondingly inward manner: through the kind of prayer that flows out of a conscience cleansed by the death and exaltation of Jesus appropriated through the response of faith.

The ultimate significance of prayer for the vision of the spiritual life contained in Hebrews is apparent in the author's understanding of the communal dimension of prayer. A consistent feature of the Christology of Hebrews is that Jesus is the beneficent Son of God, who even in his exalted state is ready to help the faithful. The same emphasis appears in the gospel narratives, which present Jesus going the way of the cross as a direct consequence of his commitment to serve others in a self-sacrificial way. This may explain why the author of Hebrews apparently works from the assumption that prayer is an activity that not only enables the encounter with God but also cultivates true mutuality between persons as a result of unimpeded access to God. To put this in somewhat different terms, the encounter with God achieved through prayer is apparently perfected for our author only when it is lived out in acts of compassionate mutuality within a communal setting. An authentic Christian spirituality cannot, therefore, be private; it necessarily involves not only a relationship with

---

[38] Koester, *Hebrews*, 550.

God but also a relationship with the Other, who in this case is the *human* Other. It is likely not an accident, then, that a call "to do good and share what you have, for such sacrifices are pleasing to God," follows immediately after the author's reference to a sacrifice of praise (13:15). According to the author of Hebrews the act of prayer apparently contributes to the transformation of the members of the community. On the basis of the strength of their relationship with God that they cultivate through prayer, the faithful are enabled to attend to others in the community in a self-sacrificial manner (see 6:10; 13:1-3), while keeping their eyes on their transcendent hope.

Chapter 4

Scripture and the Task of Identity Formation

In the previous chapter, I noted that one of the distinctive ways in which the author of Hebrews employs Scripture is in the service of shaping the identity of his audience. To that end, the author draws the attention of his auditors to the paradigmatic experience of the ancient Israelites during the Exodus in order to dissuade the community from imitating the disobedience of the wilderness generation (4:1-2). Moreover, the author uses this same story to place before the imagination of the community a vision of the glorious destiny of eternal rest that awaits them, provided that its members do not fall away from God through disbelief (3:12). Such exhortations serve a function that goes beyond the obvious motivation of providing hope and admonition to a socially marginalized community; they also contribute to the author's highly intentional task of forming his listeners into certain kinds of people—namely, persons of faith.

While the theme of faith/faithfulness appears frequently in Hebrews, the most explicit reflections on the nature of faith appear in chapter 11 of the letter. Employing wave-like crescendos of praise, the author celebrates in this section of Hebrews the ways in which numerous heroes and heroines of ancient Israel's past demonstrated the response of faith in their own lives. At the risk of oversimplifying this complex section of the letter, it seems clear that a principal aim of the author in introducing these figures is to invite his listeners to see themselves in the stories of those who struggled long ago to preserve their countercultural commitment to God. By inviting his audience to eavesdrop on the praise of these figures, the author hopes to inspire his listeners to emulate such an esteemed "cloud of witnesses," (12:1) and to think of themselves as belonging "not among those who shrink back and so are lost, but among those who have faith and so are saved" (11:39). Hence, through the challenging work of cultivating in their own lives the attitudes and behaviors of such faithful persons from the past, the community can make concrete progress in their journey on the way to heavenly rest.

The author commences his encomium on faith by presenting the community with a summary definition of what faith ultimately amounts to. We learn that faith chiefly implies, for our author, a response of confident trust that unseen realities are true despite their invisibility in the present (11:3; 11:7-8; 11:10; 11:13; 11:26). Second, and just as importantly, the response of faith judges such unseen realties as superior to present circumstances. This particular feature of faith is demonstrated most vividly by the examples of Abraham and Moses—both of whom are described as persons who interpreted the challenging circumstances of their lives in light of an unseen and far nobler reality authored by God. In the case of Abraham, that unseen reality included descendants (11:12) and ultimately a heavenly homeland (11:10, 16). In the case of Moses, the unseen reality was solidarity with the marginalized people of God (11:23-24). The community's own painful experiences with persecution at the hands of the dominant Greco-Roman culture obviously inform this understanding of faith.

With this dual definition of faith in place, one by one the author brings forward for the "edification"[1] of his audience foundational figures from Israel's past, who all serve as exemplars of the authentic response of faith. Included among these exemplars is the provocative figure of Abel. Abel is distinctive among the author's list of biblical heroes in that his name appears first in the catalogue of praise and then appears again for a second time in chapter 12 (12:24). In the author's first reference to Abel, it is the faith of the primordial brother that is emphasized—a faith that the author

---

[1] Mitchell, *Hebrews*, 231.

provocatively describes as still speaking, even up to the present day (11:4). In the second reference to Abel, the author draws a mysterious connection between the blood of Abel and the blood of Jesus. Once again the metaphor of speech makes an appearance in the text: "But you have come to Mount Zion and to the city of the living God, the heavenly Jerusalem . . . and to Jesus, the mediator of a new covenant, and to the sprinkled blood that speaks better than the blood of Abel" (12:22-24). In what follows I intend to explore the understanding of faith articulated in Hebrews by focusing on the evident christological connection that the author draws between the images of the blood of Jesus and the blood of Abel. My essential argument is that the figure of Abel functions in Hebrews as yet another way in which the author creatively emphasizes the faithful response of Jesus—a response we have seen to be central to the spirituality of the letter.

Pamela Eisenbaum notes the divergent manner in which the author of Hebrews treats the scriptural figure of Abel in Hebrews 11:4 and 12:24, respectively. She observes that, while both passages associate the theme of Abel's speech with his death, only Hebrews 12:24 seems to draw attention to the violence of Abel's death by formulating a comparison between the blood of Abel and the blood of Jesus.[2] Adding further complexity to the depiction of Abel in Hebrews is the elusiveness of a metaphor that envisions the "sprinkled blood" of Jesus as speaking better than Abel (12:24).[3] A question frequently posed by commentators concerns how precisely the blood of Jesus is understood by the author to speak better than Abel? Some have argued that the emphasis the author places on the superiority of the blood of Jesus stems from the author's conviction that reconciliation with God ensues from the event of the sacrificial death of the Son. According to this view, while the death of Jesus accomplishes reconciliation, peace, and blessing, Abel's death continually cries out for justice, vindication,

---

[2] Eisenbaum, *Jewish Heroes*, 149.
[3] Attridge, *Epistle*, 377.

and perhaps even retribution.[4] Others explain the motif of the superiority of the blood of Jesus as functioning instead to illustrate the idea of complete atonement. Support for this interpretation can be found in such passages as Hebrews 9:26, where the author links the event of the death of Jesus with the removal of sin. On this reading, the blood of Abel inscribes the primordial victim of murder as the first of numerous innocent martyrs, whose violent deaths are understood to have an atoning effect.[5] The blood of Jesus is understood to be superior, therefore, in the sense that it is more far reaching or complete in its atoning outcome.[6]

To the extent that both of these readings call attention to the strongly sacrificial setting of the Christology of the letter, they each represent a plausible interpretation of Hebrews 12:24. However, by focusing too exclusively on either the redemptive or atoning effects of Jesus' death, proponents of both models neglect the highly personalized portrait of Jesus, which, as we have seen, constitutes an important aspect of the Christology of Hebrews. In this, the concluding chapter of this study, I suggest that the elusiveness of the metaphor of blood speaking in Hebrews 12:24 is better explained by the proposal that the author is engaged in this passage with an implicit assessment of the interior disposition or character of Jesus. Through an exegetical analysis of key sections of the letter, as well as of relevant sections from the writings of the Jewish philosopher Philo of Alexandria, I shall argue that the metaphor of blood speaking provides a clue into the author's evaluative assessment of the character of the one who makes an offering. Jesus' blood (e.g., his death) is better because of the *kind* of high priest the author understands Jesus to be—namely, a high priest whose human career was characterized by a radical response of fidelity before God.

---

[4] This view has most recently been proposed by John Byron. See John Byron, "Abel's Blood and the Ongoing Cry for Vengeance," *CBQ* 73 (2011): 743–56. See also Paul Ellingworth, *The Epistle to the Hebrews: A Commentary on the Greek Text*, NIGTC (Grand Rapids: Eerdmans, 1993), 682.

[5] For the Jewish background to this understanding of atonement see 4 Macc 6:28; 17:21-22.

[6] See Attridge, *Epistle*, 377; Mitchell, *Hebrews*, 284; Koester, *Hebrews*, 546.

Abel as Paradigm for Innocent Suffering

To the disappointment of many in both the world of antiquity as well as the modern period, the Jewish Bible yields no clear explanation for the favorable judgment ascribed to the offering of Abel.[7] The account reads:

> Now Abel was a keeper of sheep, and Cain a tiller of the ground. In the course of time Cain brought to the LORD an offering of the fruit of the ground, and Abel for his part brought of the firstlings of his flock, their fat portions. And the LORD had regard for Abel and his offering, but for Cain and his offering he had no regard. So Cain was very angry, and his countenance fell. The LORD said to Cain, "Why are you angry, and why has your countenance fallen? If you do well, will you not be accepted? And if you do not do well, sin is lurking at the door; its desire is for you, but you must master it. (Gen 4:2-5)

At least as early as the Greek translation of the Septuagint, one sees an attempt to resolve the ambiguity of the Cain and Abel account preserved in the original Hebrew of the Jewish Bible. Joel Lohr, for example, helpfully draws attention to significant translations in the Septuagint that reveal a tendency to assess the offerings of Cain and Abel in an evaluative manner in order to justify the favorable selection of Abel's offering.[8] Lohr shows that, while the Jewish Bible consistently employs the Hebrew word *mincha* as a designation for the offering of both Cain and Abel, the Greek translation found in the Septuagint translates the *mincha* of Cain as a *thusia* or "sacrifice." Abel's offering, by contrast, is specified in the Septuagint as a *dōron* or "gift." [9] This difference is significant, since elsewhere in the Greek translation of Genesis the Hebrew word *mincha* is translated as *dōron* (Gen 32:14, 19, 21, 22; 33:10; 43:11, 15, 25, 26).[10] Lohr also observes that, according to the

---

[7] See Ellingworth, *Epistle*, 571.

[8] Joel N. Lohr, "Righteous Abel, Wicked Cain: Genesis 4:1-6 in the Masoretic Text, the Septuagint, and the New Testament," *CBQ* 71 (2009): 485–96.

[9] Ibid., 486–87.

[10] Ibid., 487.

Hebrew Bible, God is said to "gaze" (Gen 4:4) and not to gaze on the offerings of Abel and Cain, respectively. In the Septuagint, however, two different Greek verbs appear: God is said to "look upon" (Gen 4:4) Abel and his gifts, while God "pays no attention" (Gen 4:5) to the sacrifice offered by Cain. Lohr finds the application of these discrete verbs noteworthy, since the Septuagint frequently employs the Greek verb meaning to "look upon" to suggest the idea of God regarding one with favor.[11] Such variance in translation apparently signals ancient discomfort with a portrait of God who appears to play favorites in a disturbingly arbitrary fashion.

R. Walter L. Moberly argues that this kind of interpretive move to rationalize God's favorable assessment of Abel misses, however, the deeper theological point of the account as it is narrated in the Jewish Bible.[12] According to Moberly, the story of the primordial brothers intends to probe the mystery of divine choosing quite apart from the question of merit. In Moberly's view, therefore, the Cain and Abel story is decidedly forward looking in the sense that the narrative invites the reader to reflect on the question of what course to take whenever one faces unfair distribution in life.[13] Lohr offers a different assessment, although like Moberly he also sees the point of the Cain and Abel story as focusing squarely on the figure of Cain and the crisis of discernment he must face. Viewing Abel as a literary type of the motif of the favored latter-born son, Lohr contends that the morally ambiguous account present in the Jewish Bible affords the reader an opportunity to reflect in more complex ways on the fate of a character deemed to be an outsider, although not a completely forsaken outsider.[14]

Recently Tom Thatcher has proposed that the use of the figure of Abel in several New Testament texts demonstrates a concern

---

[11] Ibid.

[12] R. Walter L. Moberly, "Exemplars of Faith in Hebrews 11: Abel," in *The Epistle to the Hebrews and Christian Theology*, ed. Richard Bauckham, Daniel R. Driver, Trevor A. Hart and Nathan MacDonald (Grand Rapids: Eerdmans, 2009), 356.

[13] Moberly, "Exemplars," 356.

[14] Lohr, "Righteous Abel," 495–96.

for the task of communal identity formation.[15] In connection with Hebrews, he argues that the experiences of social persecution evident in the letter become meaningful by association with Abel, who functions for the audience of Hebrews as the paradigmatic innocent victim.[16] By merely mentioning Abel, the author of Hebrews prompts its auditors to make their own contemporary story of persecution for their commitment to God a reenactment of Cain's persecution of Abel, who was slain precisely because of his commitment to God.[17] Thatcher argues that the author amplifies the Septuagint's assumption of a superior sacrifice on the part of Abel by "extending" Abel's sacrifice in "explicit Christian terms," as a response of faith, which in Hebrews amounts to a bold countercultural commitment to Jesus.[18]

Thatcher's proposal is insightful. Not only does it complement a broad trend observable in the literature of the second temple period that emphasizes the righteous character of Abel,[19] but it also takes seriously the evident experiences of social dislocation borne by at least some among the audience of Hebrews. While Thatcher is correct in his assumption that communal identity formation is a feature of what we might call the historical situation of Hebrews, his specific proposal that the author of Hebrews employs the figure of Abel to address the traumatic experience of persecution is not completely persuasive in my judgment. The following two examples illustrate the limitations of Thatcher's proposal. First, while Hebrews 12:24 presupposes the violent death of Abel, the author of Hebrews actually shows little explicit interest in developing this aspect of the Abel story. This fact becomes all the more striking when one considers that our author's focus on the speech of Abel clearly derives from the notice in the

---

[15] Tom Thatcher, "Cain and Abel in Early Christian Memory: A Case Study in the Use of the Old Testament in the New," *CBQ* 72 (2010): 732–51.

[16] Ibid., 743.

[17] Ibid., 745.

[18] Thatcher's use of the term "Christian" both here and elsewhere in his article is somewhat anachronistic, since it implies a confessional identity that goes beyond the evidence of the text of Hebrews.

[19] See Matt 23:35; Luke 11:51; *Hel. Syn. Pr.* 6:4; *Asc. Isa.* 9:8; *Q.G. 1.70*; *T. 12 Patr.* 5.5.

Jewish Bible concerning how Abel's blood cried out to God from the ground (Gen 4:10). Hebrews, however, does not exploit the fact that Abel was murdered, even though this might have complemented other passages in the letter where the author has in view the unjust abuse borne by Jesus (see 12:3). Nor does the author ever present Abel as a figure seeking vindication or justice for his murder.[20] In the narrative world of Hebrews it is consistently God who is depicted as a judgment figure (see 4:12-13; 10:26-31). The surrounding context of 12:24 dwells instead on the theme of the heavenly homeland that the author insists the community has already approached as a result of the faithful death of Jesus. With all this in mind, I think it is more correct to maintain that Abel functions for our author less as a figure who legitimates the experience of suffering that is somehow integral to "Christian" identity[21] and more as an example of the first righteous person to enter into the divine realm.[22] Such an assessment coheres with both the emphasis that the author places on the heavenly homeland which will be the destiny for those in the community who endure, as well as the repeated affirmation in the letter that Jesus has entered into heaven, indeed into the very presence of God (6:19-20; 7:26; 8:1; 9:12, 24; 10:12).[23] Second, in 11:4 the author is concerned with the event that precedes Abel's murder—namely, the superior or greater sacrifice that Abel offered to God in faith. While this passage likely does take for granted the memory of the death of Abel, little prominence is given to the violent persecution

---

[20] See Anthony Hilhorst, "Abel's Speaking in Hebrews 11:4 and 12:24," in *Eve's Children: The Biblical Stories Retold and Interpreted in Jewish and Christian Traditions*, ed. Gerhard P. Luttikhuizen, Themes in Biblical Narrative 5 (Leiden: Brill, 2003), 119–27.

[21] Thatcher, "Cain and Abel," 744.

[22] Thatcher makes a brief reference to this theme in a footnote, but he unfortunately does not elaborate on it. See Thatcher, "Cain and Abel," 744 n. 32. See also Eisenbaum, *Jewish Heroes*, 149.

[23] With such observations in mind, we might say that the figure of Abel functions in Hebrews in part as a comparative backdrop both for the event of Jesus' exaltation and the theme of the heavenly destiny for the faithful. While certain Second Temple Jewish texts such as 1 Enoch 22 depict Abel as alive in some sense, in Hebrews the exalted life of Jesus is such that the Son enters the very presence of God (Heb 9:24), a destiny that is also available to the auditors of the letter (4:16; 10:19).

of Abel *per se*.[24] What does appear in view in Hebrews 11:4 is an implicit assessment of the interior disposition or character of Abel, as suggested by the author's claim that Abel performed a sacrifice by means of the response of faith. Given that (1) the author of Hebrews also praises Jesus for his response of faithfulness (2:17; 3:2) and that (2) the comparison between Abel and Jesus focuses on the superior blood of Jesus, it makes better sense, I would argue, to locate the possible meaning of Hebrews 12:24 against the more immediate background of the Christology of the letter. In what follows I hope to demonstrate that a hallmark of this Christology is a focus on the radical and highly personal character of Jesus' response of fidelity before God.

The Function of the Speech of Jesus in the Christology of Hebrews

One of the striking verbal links connecting Hebrews 11:4 and 12:24 is a shared emphasis on the act of speech. Hence, in 11:4 the author depicts Abel in some sense speaking although he has died, while in 12:24 it is the blood of Jesus that is understood to speak. A common reading of 11:4 takes the postmortem speech of Abel as the voice of a martyr seeking retribution for an unjust death.[25] Literary support for this appraisal appears in the form of brief notices from such second-temple Jewish texts as Jubilees 4:3-4 and 1 Enoch 22:7, which both present Abel as appealing for justice against his elder brother.[26] Other scholars, however, find more persuasive the proposal offered by James Moffatt, who argued long ago that the reference to the speech of Abel in 11:4 functions as scriptural testimony of an example of fidelity to be emulated

---

[24] Eisenbaum (*Jewish Heroes*, 148) notes that not every figure in Hebrews 11 is a martyr or remembered for suffering.

[25] See Attridge, *Epistle*, 317; Herbert Braun, *An die Hebräer*, HNT 14 (Tübingen: Mohr Siebeck, 1984), 345; Ceslas Spicq, *L'Épître aux Hébreux*, 2 vols. (Paris: Gabalda, 1952/53), 342–43; Ellingworth, *Epistle*, 573; Hilhorst, "Abel's Speaking," 127.

[26] See also Philo, *Det*. 49.

by later readers.[27] Pamela Eisenbaum offers two compelling reasons for the cogency of this latter reading. First, she notes that Hebrews begins in 1:1 with the author contrasting the speech of God that is centered personally in a Son with the divine revelation located in the scriptural witness. While the author understands God to speak in both cases, it seems clear that the association of the last days with the Son lends an eschatological climax to the motif of God's speech. Second, while conceding that the scriptural referent of 11:4 is not immediately transparent, Eisenbaum echoes the judgment of many commentators who see, behind the image of blood that speaks (12:24), a distinct echo to Genesis 4:10, where Abel's blood is portrayed as crying out from the ground. Eisenbaum suggests that the essential contrast inherent to 12:24 is a contrast between scriptural testimony and the historical event of the life and death of Jesus.[28] In her own words, "in 12:24, the blood of Jesus speaks better than the blood of Abel, which is a specific scriptural example, and therefore does indeed have revelatory import, but nevertheless not as much as the import of Christ."[29] One of the strengths of this assessment is that it complements the role that the rhetorical device *synkrisis* plays in 12:24 and indeed throughout the theological argumentation of Hebrews (see 1:4; 3:3; 7:19, 22; 8:6).[30] As previously noted in chapter 3, ancient speakers/authors employed this rhetorical tool as a way to amplify the prestige of a subject by comparing that subject to a person whose exemplary character was evident to all. The point of the contrast in 12:24 between the blood of Jesus and Abel, therefore, is not to denigrate Abel, but to affirm that Jesus recapitulates and at the same time surpasses an attribute associated with Abel. I suggest that an examination of those passages in the letter that focus on

---

[27] See James Moffatt, *A Critical and Exegetical Commentary on the Epistle to the Hebrews* (Edinburgh: T & T Clark, 1924), 164; see also H. W. Montifiore, *A Commentary on the Epistle to the Hebrews* (London: Adam and Charles Black, 1964), 190; R. Alan Culpepper, "A Superior Faith: Hebrews 10:19-12:2," *RevExp* 82 (1985): 375–90.

[28] Eisenbaum, *Jewish Heroes*, 149.

[29] Ibid., 149 n. 62.

[30] For a recent and helpful discussion of the role of *synkrisis* in Hebrews, see James Thompson, "The New Is Better: A Neglected Aspect of the Hermeneutics of Hebrews," *CBQ* 73 (2011): 547–61.

the speech of Jesus reveals that the attribute inscribed by the metaphor of blood that speaks concerns the response of fidelity before God.

Noting the nonsystematic character of the Christology of Hebrews, Harold Attridge directs attention to several passages in the letter where the author links the portrait of Jesus as high priest to both his exalted status in heaven and to his human career on earth.[31] An examination of the latter in particular proves fruitful in terms of the evocative connection Hebrews makes between Jesus' blood and speech in 12:24. Beginning in the exordium of the letter, the author displays an obvious preoccupation with the theme of God's speech.[32] In addition to affirming that God spoke in the past and has now spoken definitively in a Son (1:1), the author also has God directly address the exalted Jesus in Hebrews 1:5 and 1:13 in the words of Psalm 2:7, 2 Samuel 7:14, and Psalm 110:1 (109:1 LXX). Less emphasized by commentators, however, are those comparatively fewer passages in the letter where Jesus addresses God directly. Hebrews 2:12-13 reads:

> "I will proclaim your name among my brothers and sisters, in the midst of the congregation I will praise you." And again, "I will put my trust in him." And again, "Here am I and the children whom God has given me."

Hebrews 2:12-13 is comprised of three separate scriptural quotations. The source for verse 12 is Psalm 22:23, while verse 13 quotes Isaiah 8:17-18. These first of Jesus' words in Hebrews are best interpreted in light of the surrounding context comprised by Hebrews 2:1-18, in which the theme of the Son's beneficent solidarity with humanity is especially evident (see 2:8-9, 11, 14, 16, 17-18).[33] Thus, the "children" (2:13-14) depicted as given to Jesus are intimately identified as Jesus' brothers and sisters (2:11-12, 17). Moreover, the true depth of the Son's involvement with humanity is

---

[31] Attridge (*Epistle*, 29) characterizes these as Christological "antinomies." The following passages provide helpful examples: 1:3-4; 4:14-15; 7:23-26; 9:24-26.

[32] See Harold W. Attridge, "God in Hebrews," in *The Epistle to the Hebrews and Christian Theology*, 103–8.

[33] See McCruden, "The Concept of Perfection," 215.

such that the Son is said to participate completely in their flesh and blood existence (2:14, 17), even to the extent of identifying with their experiences of painful testing (2:18). The depth of Jesus' involvement with humanity is signaled by the author's use of adverbial phrases. Hence, in 2:14 the author depicts Jesus as participating in the blood and flesh of humanity in "just the same way," while in 2:17 Jesus is said to resemble "in every way" the brothers and sisters. This emphasis on the theme of Jesus' solidarity with humanity prepares the reader for the first mention in the letter of the motif of the high priesthood of Jesus (2:17). Notably, the first quality that the author associates with the high priesthood of Jesus is its merciful character. Immediately following this description is the prominence given by the author to the faithfulness or fidelity of Jesus. On a rhetorical level, it is likely that Hebrews 2:12-13 bears a pastoral function in the sense that Jesus' words inscribe behavior meant to be imitated by the audience of the letter.[34] In emulation of Jesus, therefore, the auditors of Hebrews are encouraged to acknowledge publicly their commitment to God and to place their trust in God despite societal scorn.[35] Strength to imitate Jesus comes from the knowledge that, in contrast to the stance of the dominant society, Jesus is not ashamed of those who look to him as the "pioneer" of their salvation (2:10). Indeed, as a result of his commitment to, and solidarity with, the children, Jesus is a high priest who sympathizes (4:15) with their weaknesses and provides for them a model of fidelity (2:17; 3:2; 12:2; 13:13).

Arguably the key theological affirmation expressed in Hebrews 2:12-13 consists of the words of Jesus that give expression to his own commitment to God: "I will put my trust in him" (2:13b). A similar but more elaborate treatment of the theme of Jesus' commitment to God appears in 10:5-10, the passage where Jesus speaks for the second and final time in Hebrews:

Consequently, when Christ came into the world, he said, "Sacrifices and offerings you have not desired, but a body you have prepared for me; in burnt offerings and sin offerings you have

[34] See Attridge, "God in Hebrews," 105.
[35] See Koester, *Hebrews*, 238.

taken no pleasure. Then I said, 'See, God, I have come to do your will, O God' (in the scroll of the book it is written of me)." When he said above, "You have neither desired nor taken pleasure in sacrifices and offerings and burnt offerings and sin offerings" (these are offered according to the law), then he added, "See, I have come to do your will." He abolishes the first in order to establish the second. And it is by God's will that we have been sanctified through the offering of the body of Jesus Christ once for all.

In this passage the author highlights the degree to which Jesus conforms to the will of God by the twice repeated reference to Jesus' own commitment, first in 10:7 and then again in 10:9. As in 2:12-13, the content of Jesus' speech in 10:5-9 is supplied by the words of the psalmist (Ps 40:7-9). In its original context Psalm 40 celebrates the intention of the speaker to obey God's will as revealed in the Law.[36] Exploiting the prophetic contrast already contained in the psalm between sacrifice and obedience, the author focuses on the superiority of the psalmist's, e.g., Jesus' personal response.[37] The author's preoccupation with the personal response of Jesus is further demonstrated by the references to the body of Jesus in both 10:5 and 10:10, references that serve to emphasize the totality of Jesus' response of obedience or fidelity.

Hebrews 2:12-13 and 10:5-9 evince two features that prove integral to the significance of Jesus' speech for the author. First, each passage focuses strongly on the commitment of Jesus to embody God's will (2:13b; 10:7b, 9). Not to be missed, however, is the emphasis the author places on the personal quality of that commitment on the part of Jesus to attend to the will of God. Hence, 10:5 depicts God as preparing a "body" *sōma* for Jesus, while in 10:10 the author affirms for the community the complete assurance of sanctification that results "through the offering of the body of Jesus Christ once for all." Hebrews 2:12-13 also accentuates the depth of the personal commitment of Jesus, for in order to accomplish the divine intention to lead many children to glory (2:10),

[36] Attridge, *Epistle*, 274.
[37] Ibid.

Jesus is said to have participated in the blood and flesh of the children (2:14). The consequence of this commitment according to the author is the possibility for entry into God's presence (see 10:19-22; 12:22-24).

Hebrews 5:7-9 and the Voice of Jesus

Given the homiletic character of Hebrews, it is helpful to ask the question whether such passages as these that are informed by the speech of Jesus may have triggered in the minds of the audience of the letter points made earlier by the author relating to the human career of Jesus. A potential candidate that comes immediately to mind is one we have already had an opportunity to analyze at some length in chapter 2:

> In the days of his flesh, Jesus offered up prayers and supplications, with loud cries and tears, to the one who was able to save him from death, and he was heard because of his reverent submission. Although he was a Son, he learned obedience through what he suffered; and having been made perfect, he became the source of eternal salvation for all who obey him. (Heb 5:7-9)

Although the first reference to the status of Jesus as high priest occurs as early as 2:17, it is not until the second major section of the letter beginning in 4:14 that the author begins to develop the high priest title in any significant fashion. This section takes up again the topic of Jesus' solidarity with humanity by affirming the sympathetic character of the Son. Despite his exaltation into heaven (4:14), Jesus "sympathizes" with the "weaknesses" of the children, since like them he was tested during his earthly career.[38] While chapter 5 begins with the author reflecting in a general way on the qualifications of the human high priest, the argument quickly progresses to an exposition of the significance of Jesus' experience of suffering, culminating with the first mention in the

---

[38] See McCruden, "The Concept of Perfection," 220.

letter of Jesus' link with Melchizedek (5:10). As was also the case in 10:5-9 and 2:14, the incarnation of Jesus comes immediately into view in 5:7: "In the days of his flesh." Moreover, just as the author refers to the "body" of Jesus in 10:5 and 10:10, a reference to Jesus' "flesh" appears in 5:7. A strongly sacrificial but also highly personalized atmosphere animates the entire passage, since the author depicts Jesus as having offered "prayers" and "entreaties" with "loud cries and tears."

Although it would be inaccurate to maintain that the anguished emotions expressed by Jesus amount to a third instance of Jesus speaking in the letter, it is reasonable to argue that the original recipients of Hebrews may have associated the portrait of Jesus found in 5:7-9 with those passages in the sermon where Jesus directly addresses God.[39] Put in slightly different terms, while the direct speech of Jesus is absent in 5:7-9, I would want to argue that the voice of Jesus is decidedly present. Indeed the author makes a point of affirming in 5:7 that Jesus was heard, something he affirms about Jesus nowhere else in the letter. I suggest that what 2:13b states in an abstract manner—that Jesus will place his trust in God—5:7-9 elevates to more concrete expression with the dramatic portrayal of the human struggle of Jesus. Moreover, when Jesus speaks for the second time in the letter (10:5-10) and affirms his commitment to accomplish the will of God, there is likely an intended echo to the "obedience" that Jesus is said to have learned through suffering (5:9).

Admittedly, the author's insistence that Jesus was heard by God is perplexing, since it follows immediately upon the assertion that Jesus addressed the one "who was able to save him from death" (5:7). Since the author is aware of the tradition that Jesus died on the cross (6:6; 12:2), it is not clear how Jesus could have been heard by God. Scholarly opinion on this matter has largely been influenced by assumptions concerning the intended meaning of the noun translated as "reverent submission" in 5:7. Given that the same noun could be employed in contexts suggestive of caution or even

[39] For example, there is a direct verbal link between 5:7 and 10:10 in the use of the language of sacrificial offering.

anxiety,[40] some have claimed that the author believes Jesus was heard in the sense that God empowered him to overcome the fear of death.[41] However, if the author's meaning instead is that Jesus prayed not to remain in the state of death, this would imply that Jesus was heard in the sense that he was rewarded for his reverence by being exalted by God.[42] Commentators who advocate the former reading tend to read 5:7 as a kind of epitome of the Gethsemane accounts where Jesus overcomes his fear of approaching death through prayer.[43] Thus David Peterson remarks: "Our writer recalls the struggle of Jesus to do the will of God when the ordinary fear of death as the place of expulsion and God-forsakenness, tempted him to turn aside."[44] Those scholars who prefer to translate the noun as meaning reverence point to the closely adjoining reference to Jesus having been made complete or perfect, which likely does refer—at least in part—to the exaltation or glorification of Jesus.[45] This last observation—especially when coupled with Hebrews 13:20, which clearly does refer to God rescuing Jesus from the realm or state of death—appears the stronger of the two readings. That said, there may be a way of combining both interpretations in the sense that by affirming that Jesus was heard by God, the author may also be referring to the highly personal response of fidelity on the part of Jesus. On this reading, while exaltation can be taken to mean the final consequence of God's hearing of Jesus, it is actually the response of Jesus' fidelity that is of first importance for the author. What God hears and ultimately rewards, in other words, is the struggle of Jesus to embody completely and concretely his trust and commitment in God (2:13) and to accomplish God's will (10:7). Just as the author is convinced that Abel was attested as righteous by God on account of his response of faith (11:4), it is apparently Jesus' own response of fidelity (2:13;

---

[40] See Koester, *Hebrews*, 289.

[41] See Ellingworth, *Epistle*, 290.

[42] See Attridge, *Epistle*, 150; Ellingworth, *Epistle*, 290; Koester, *Hebrews*, 288.

[43] Peterson too confidently maintains that Hebrews 5:7 has Gethsemane in view. See Peterson, *Hebrews and Perfection*, 87.

[44] Ibid., 92. See also Ellingworth, *Epistle*, 290.

[45] See McCruden, "The Concept of Perfection," 215.

3:2; 10:7, 9) that the author sees as attested by God in the sense of being heard. If this reading is a plausible one, then it may be not too far off to maintain that Hebrews works with a similar narrative understanding of the Christ event, as is visible in the Philippians hymn (Phil 2:6-11). By utilizing the verb *phroneō* at the beginning of the hymn (Phil 2:5), Paul prefaces the lines that follow with what we might characterize as a clear pastoral orientation by focusing on the disposition or attitude of Jesus. The cumulative effect of the verbs that Paul employs in verses 6-8 focuses the attention of the reader on the attitude and actions of Jesus, which lead ultimately to his death (2:8). With the comment in 2:9 that God highly exalted Jesus, the effect on the reader is to perceive God's action as an explicit response to Jesus' act of selfless obedience. To employ a metaphor from Hebrews, we might say that in Philippians 2:9, God hears Jesus much as Jesus is said to be heard in Hebrews 5:7.

The Eloquent Blood of Jesus

In an important essay dealing with the topic of moral formation in the writings of Philo of Alexandria, Hindy Najman examines Philo's treatment of the Cain and Abel story through the lens of character analysis.[46] Noting the frequency with which Philo in his ethical reflections employs the term *typos* (mark, impression, stamp), Najman suggests that this term functions for Philo in the sense of a disposition to act in a particular way—namely, a character trait.[47] In the broadest sense, Cain represents for Philo the character trait of wickedness, while Abel represents the trait of piety (*Questions and Answers on Genesis*, 59, 61). On the anthropological level, however, Philo considers both of these traits to be potentialities contained with the human soul that can either be strengthened by virtuous action or destroyed by transgression (*On the Sacrifices of Cain and Abel*, 2–4; *Det.* 49).[48]

---

[46] Hindy Najman, "Cain and Abel as Character Traits: A Study in the Allegorical Typology of Philo of Alexandria," in *Eve's Children*, 107–18.

[47] Ibid., 111.

[48] Ibid., 111–13.

Several of the observations of Philo concerning the interior dispositions of the two brothers prove suggestive when read in light of the analysis above relating to the highly personalized account of Jesus' commitment to God. For example, Philo notes the following: "Such were the charges brought against Cain who made his offering after many days. But Abel brought other offerings, and in other manner. His offering was "living," Cain's was "lifeless" (*Sacr.* 88). Philo's initial criticism of Cain is of a temporal character. Essentially, Cain takes his precious time in the discharging of his offering. From the standpoint of character analysis, however, Philo's second accusation is the more substantive of the two, for he states that while the offerings of Abel were living, the offering of Cain was not. Philo makes a similar observation in *Questions and Answers on Genesis*, in which he contends that, while Abel traded in living creatures, Cain devoted himself to inanimate objects (*Q.G.* 59).[49]

Hebrews strikes a similar note when, at the conclusion of the elaborate treatment of the priestly offering of Jesus in 10:19-23, the author celebrates, among other things, the "new" and "living" access to God made possible by the sacrificial death of Jesus. The author's emphasis on the living quality of such access to God actually echoes a theme expressed most clearly in Hebrews 9:11-14:

> But when Christ came as a high priest of the good things that
> have come, then through the greater and perfect tent (not made
> with hands, that is, not of this creation), he entered once for all
> into the Holy Place, not with the blood of goats and calves, but
> with his own blood, thus obtaining an eternal redemption. For
> if the blood of goats and bulls, with the sprinkling of the ashes
> of a heifer, sanctifies those who have been defiled so that their
> flesh is purified, how much more will the blood of Christ, who

[49] This appraisal of the offerings of the two brothers is also present in the writings of the Jewish historian Josephus: "This was the offering which found more favour with God, who is honored by things that grow spontaneously and in accordance with natural laws, and not by the products forced from nature by the ingenuity of grasping man" (*Ant* I.54).

through the eternal Spirit offered himself without blemish to God, purify our conscience from dead works to worship the living God!

Hebrews 9:11-14 appears in a section of the letter (7:15-9:10) where the author quite heavily emphasizes the theme of the eternal character of Jesus' high priesthood (7:16, 24; 8:2; 9:23-24). At the same time, however, what apparently makes Jesus' priestly activity superior to the Levitical priesthood in this passage is the personalized character of his sacrifice. Put another way, the sacrificial death of Jesus is superior for the author, at least in part, because Jesus offers his own blood (9:12). It is important to note that this emphasis on the personal quality of Jesus' sacrifice is by no means an isolated one in the letter. For example, in addition to assuring the community that the blood of Jesus has opened a new and living way into the sanctuary of God (10:19), the author locates sanctification in the offering of the body of Jesus (10:10) and precisely not in the blood of bulls and goats (10:4). Moreover, the author makes a point of saying that the Levitical high priest, in contrast to Jesus, enters the holy place with blood that is not his own (9:25).

   Attention to this highly personalized assessment of Jesus' sacrificial activity may also help to clarify the ambiguous reference to "eternal spirit" that appears in connection with the offering of Jesus in 9:14. Since the author has referred earlier to the Holy Spirit (2:4; 3:7; 6:4; 9:8; 10:15) some think the reference in 9:14 to "eternal spirit" is to the Holy Spirit.[50] Kenneth Schenck helpfully points out, however, that while the author can employ the Greek word *pneuma* to refer to the Holy Spirit (3:7; 9:8; 10:15), he likewise can employ *pneuma* as a designation for the most inward part of a

---

[50] See Barnabas Lindars, *The Theology*, 58; see also F. F. Bruce, *The Epistle to the Hebrews*, NICNT (Grand Rapids, Eerdmans, 1975), 205; Lane, *Hebrews*, 2. 240; O'Brien, *Letter to the Hebrews*, 324. Brooke Foss Westcott (*The Epistle to the Hebrews: The Greek Text with Notes and Essays* (London: Macmillan, 1889), 261, echoes an earlier patristic evaluation that views the phrase "eternal spirit" as indicative of Jesus' divine nature. But this is to read a later doctrinal development into the author's Christology.

person (4:12; 12:23).[51] Since many of the author's references to the Holy Spirit are linked with scriptural citation, Schenck prefers to see the reference to "eternal Spirit" without the article as denoting the eternal spirit of Jesus.[52] Noting the emphasis placed by the author on the eternal nature of Jesus' priesthood, Schenck proposes that what ultimately makes Jesus' sacrifice greater is its heavenly character.[53] But this is to miss the author's consistent emphasis on the deeply personal element of Jesus' obedience conveyed by the image of Jesus' blood (9:12, 25; 10:4). The sacrificial death of Jesus has revelatory import for the author not in the sense that it is accomplished in heaven but because the blood of Jesus that was shed in the course of living out God's will led to eternal redemption (9:12). What the author seems to be suggesting is that Jesus' response of fidelity was so radical and personal that it engenders an eternal significance from the perspective of God.[54] While Schenck is most likely correct that the phrase "eternal spirit" refers to the personhood of Jesus, his stress on the eternal nature of that personhood is probably mistaken. Luke Timothy Johnson perhaps comes closest to the probable force of the author's use of "eternal spirit" when he notes that the phrase likely points in some way to what we might characterize as the "internal disposition" of Jesus.[55] Noting the author's description in the same verse of Jesus' offering of himself as "blameless," Johnson sees the reference to "eternal spirit" as a kind of shorthand for expressing the idea of the integrity and innocence of Jesus.[56] In a similar fashion, Attridge understands the author's meaning to be that the self-offering of Jesus according to Hebrews was made with that "por-

---

[51] Kenneth Schenck, *Understanding the Book of Hebrews: The Story Behind the Sermon* (Louisville: Westminster John Knox Press, 2003), 83.

[52] Ibid., 82–83.

[53] Ibid., 82–83.

[54] Attridge (*Epistle*, 269) states of the sacrificial activity of Jesus in Hebrews that it "consists not simply in its physical quality, but in the willingness with which it was made. Hence, it is the interior disposition of the act that makes it the heavenly or spiritual event that our author holds it to be."

[55] Johnson, *Hebrews*, 238.

[56] Ibid. See also Moffat, *Hebrews*, 124.

tion of his being that was most truly himself."[57] Both of these readings of the phrase "eternal spirit" are consonant with what we have seen to be a consistent feature of the Christocentric spirituality of Hebrews: a focus on the faithful disposition or faithful character of Jesus.

An analysis of Hebrews 2:12-13, 5:7-9, 10:5-10, and finally 9:11-14 in conjunction with several suggestive passages from Philo, calls for Hebrews 12:24 to be viewed in a new light. As described above, the metaphor of blood speaking in 12:24 may very well have echoed in the minds of at least some among Hebrews' audience certain other passages in the letter where either the speech or the voice of Jesus gives expression to the theme of Jesus' radical fidelity before God. Much as Philo celebrates Abel as being completely devoted to God (*Det.* 32; *Q.G.* I. 60), the author of Hebrews presents Jesus as the Son who "offered" personal tears and cries as a form of embodied "reverent submission" with regard to God's will. Moreover, in a manner analogous to Abel, who offered a "living" sacrifice (*Sacr.* 88), Jesus inaugurates in Hebrews a "new" and "living" way into the presence of God as a consequence of offering his own blood. With these observations in mind, the christological logic of the particular form of *synkrisis* integral to 12:24 becomes more apparent. When the author declares in 12:24 that the blood of Jesus speaks better than the blood of Abel, his point seems to be that Jesus' embodied life of fidelity recapitulates and surpasses the fidelity of Abel that the author sees as forever attested to in Scripture (11:4).

Readings, therefore, that locate the comparison between Jesus and Abel exclusively against the background of atonement reflection miss the implicit attention that Hebrews 12:24 gives to the theme of the fidelity of Jesus. Too little consideration has been given to the question of how the metaphor of blood that speaks might relate to other passages in the letter where either the voice of Jesus is in view or where the author emphasizes the personal dimension of the response of Jesus' faithfulness before God. Twice in Hebrews the author depicts Jesus as addressing God, and in

---

[57] Attridge, *Epistle*, 251.

each of these instances the fidelity of Jesus appears as a consistent theme. Given the author's notice that Jesus was heard by God (5:7), we have also considered how Hebrews 5:7-9 likely amounts to a third instance in the letter where at least the voice of Jesus is in view. The author of Hebrews undoubtedly shared the traditional assessment widely attested in the second temple period that Abel was righteous and approved by God. Likely by exploiting the link between the themes of righteousness and faith found in Habakkuk (10:38), the author reworks the similarly traditional assessment of the fidelity of Jesus primarily through the thematic medium of the speech and voice of Jesus. The metaphor of blood that speaks in 12:24 captures in a highly evocative sense what the author of Hebrews understands as the full embodiment of fidelity intimated in the scriptural witness to Abel.

Conclusion

As we look back over the four chapters comprising this study, it is my hope that I have successfully illustrated for the reader some of the key dimensions of what I have described as the spirituality of Hebrews. I began this study by offering a relatively straightforward definition of spirituality as indicative of the idea of the luminescence of the transcendent within concrete human experience. Guided by this definition of the spiritual life, I have attempted to demonstrate how the Christology of Hebrews—and in particular Hebrews's portrait of Jesus as a perfect high priest—captures both poles of this definition. The emphasis one encounters in Hebrews on the surpassing value of transcendent reality has been readily and repeatedly observed by many. Frequently less noted, however, is the sustained attention the author gives to the human response of Jesus involved in the Son's living out the will of God (5:7; 10:7).

Whenever I read Hebrews I am frequently reminded of that dramatic scene narrated in the Synoptic Gospels of Matthew and Luke where Jesus is said to be led by God's Spirit into the wilderness to endure a period of testing (Matt 4:1-11; Luke 4:1-13). While this scene is likely a legendary story that developed at least in part out of the memory that Jesus was a powerful exorcist, the testing story nonetheless reveals an important claim that the early Christians wanted to make about Jesus concerning the shape of his human career. In both versions of the testing story Jesus appears as the Son of God who is completely transparent to the will of God for his life. For this reason, for example, Jesus disavows the seductive and ultimately demonic offer of wielding power over others (Matt 4:8-10; Luke 4:5-8) in preparation for the life of countercultural service to others that will characterize his historical ministry.

According to the Synoptic Gospels, it is precisely this commitment on the part of Jesus to live a life of cruciform commitment to others in obedience to God's will that leads ultimately to his death. Such at least seems to be the import of passages such as Mark 8:34 where we see Jesus offer the following teaching lesson to his disciples: "If any want to become my followers, let them deny themselves and take up their cross and follow me. For those who want to save their life will lose it, and those who lose their life for my sake, and for the sake of the gospel, will save it." In commenting on this passage, Elizabeth Struthers Malbon makes this important observation: "Crucifixion was for those challenging the Roman authority, challenging the status quo of the powerful. And Jesus says, 'That's what you have to be willing to do. . . . For those who want to save their lives will end up losing them, and those willing to lose their lives—not for no reason, but for my sake and for the sake of the good news of God's in-breaking kingdom—will in fact find their lives.'"[1] This passage appears in a specific section of Mark's narrative where Jesus repeatedly tries to teach his disciples about the necessity for living in countercultural ways if they are to authentically follow Jesus, the Son of man who "came not to be served, but to serve, and to give his life as a ransom for many" (Mark 10:45). According to the gospels, Jesus is unjustly executed as a result of living out to the fullest his commitment to such a life. And according to the gospels, God validates this commitment by ultimately raising Jesus from the dead. As the author of Hebrews notes, God heard Jesus (5:7), the same Jesus who "endured the cross, disregarding its shame" (12:2).

We have seen that, in a manner similar to the anonymous author of Mark's gospel, the anonymous author of Hebrews is also committed to the idea that the person of Jesus reveals the pattern of what a human life might look like that is lived in light of the transcendent presence of God's will. Our author was heir to traditional appraisals about Jesus that stressed the faithfulness (3:6) of Jesus, the righteousness of Jesus (1:9), as well as the sinlessness of Jesus

---

[1] Elizabeth Struthers Malbon, *Hearing Mark: A Listener's Guide* (Harrisburg: Trinity Press, 2002), 59.

(4:15; 7:26). We have seen that each of these appraisals is concerned largely with the faith commitment that Jesus demonstrated perfect obedience to God throughout his entire life. The author of Hebrews would have his audience understand that Jesus was exalted into heaven, indeed into the very presence of God (9:24), precisely as a result of the shape of the Son's faithful human career. As Hebrews 12:23 suggests, even now the faithful righteous ones of Israel's past celebrated in Hebrews 11:1-40, are presently waiting to welcome the similarly challenged and beleaguered faithful ones who comprise the community addressed in this sermon.

A central claim I have made repeatedly in this study is that Hebrews was written for a community of early Christians who had experienced the painful effects of social and even physical marginalization as a result of their countercultural commitment to Jesus. The author is well aware of the potentially debilitating effects such experiences can exert on the will to persevere. By presenting Jesus as someone who was both tested by sufferings (2:18; 5:8) and opposed by others (12:3), the author offers his audience what I have described in chapter 1 as a countercultural vantage point from which to interpret their challenging social circumstances. Assured of the heavenly reward that Jesus received as a result of his own expression of human faithfulness, the community addressed in Hebrews is invited by the author to pursue a similar path in their own lives. Not a little part of the rhetorical richness of this invitation lies in the creative way in which the author employs a Christocentric spirituality, which reflects on how the human Jesus modeled the luminescence of the transcendent in the concrete circumstances of his own life.

Bibliography

Attridge, Harold W. *The Epistle to the Hebrews: A Commentary on the Epistle to the Hebrews*. Hermeneia. Philadelphia: Fortress Press, 1989.

————. " 'Let Us Strive to Enter That Rest': The Logic of Hebrews 4:1-11." *Harvard Theological Review* 73 (1980): 279–88.

————. "God in Hebrews." In *The Epistle to the Hebrews and Christian Theology*. Edited by Richard Bauckham, Daniel R. Driver, Trevor A. Hart, and Nathan MacDonald. Grand Rapids: Eerdmans, 2009, pp. 95–110.

Aune, David E. *The New Testament in Its Literary Environment*. Library of Early Christianity. Philadelphia: Westminster Press, 1987.

Bassler, Jouette M. *Navigating Paul: An Introduction to Key Theological Concepts*. Louisville: Westminster John Knox Press, 2007.

Braun, Herbert. *An die Hebräer*. Handbuch zum Neuen Testament 14. Tübingen: Mohr Siebeck, 1984.

Brown, Raymond E. *Birth of the Messiah: A Commentary on the Infancy Narratives in Matthew and Luke*. New York: Doubleday, 1977.

Bruce, F. F. *The Epistle to the Hebrews*. New International Commentary on the New Testament. Grand Rapids: Eerdmans, 1975.

Bultmann, Rudolph. *Theology of the New Testament*. 2 vols. Translated by Kendrick Grobel. New York: Charles Scribner's Sons, 1951.

Byron, John. "Abel's Blood and the Ongoing Cry for Vengeance." *Catholic Biblical Quarterly* 73 (2011): 743–56.

Culpepper, R. Alan. "A Superior Faith: Hebrews 10:19-12:2." *Review and Expositor* 82 (1985): 375–90.

Cunningham, Lawrence S. and Keith J. Egan. *Christian Spirituality: Themes from the Tradition*. New Jersey: Paulist Press, 1996.

DeSilva, David A. "Entering God's Rest: Eschatology and the Socio-Historical Strategy of Hebrews." *Trinity Journal* 21 (2000): 25–43.

———. *The Letter to the Hebrews in Social Science Perspective.* Eugene, OR: Cascade, 2012.

Docherty, Susan E. *The Use of the Old Testament in Hebrews: A Case Study in Early Jewish Bible Interpretation.* Wissenschaftliche Untersuchungen zum Neuen Testament 2, no. 260. Tübingen: Mohr Siebeck, 2009.

Downey, Michael. *Understanding Christian Spirituality.* New Jersey: Paulist Press, 1997.

Dunn, James D. G. *The Theology of Paul the Apostle.* Grand Rapids: Eerdmans, 1998.

Eisenbaum, Pamela M. *Paul Was Not a Christian: The Original Message of a Misunderstood Apostle.* New York: Harper, 2009.

———. *The Jewish Heroes of Christian History: Hebrews 11 in Literary Context.* Society of Biblical Literature Dissertation Series 156. Atlanta: Scholars Press, 1997.

Ellingworth, Paul. *The Epistle to the Hebrews: A Commentary on the Greek Text.* New International Greek Testament Commentary. Grand Rapids: Eerdmans, 1993.

Exupéry, Antoine de Saint. *The Little Prince.* Translated by Katherine Woods. San Diego: Harvest, 1971.

Gleason, Randall C. "The Old Testament Background of Rest in Hebrews 3:7–4:11." *Bibliotheca Sacra* 57 (2000): 281–303.

Goodman, Martin D. *The Ruling Class of Judea: The Origin of the Jewish Revolt against Rome A.D. 66–70.* Cambridge: Cambridge University Press, 1987.

Gorman, Michael J. *Apostle of the Crucified Lord: A Theological Introduction to Paul & His Letters.* Grand Rapids: Eerdmans, 2004.

Gray, Patrick. "Hebrews among Greeks and Romans." In *Reading the Epistle to the Hebrews: A Resource for Students.* Society of Biblical Literature Resources for Biblical Study 66. Edited by Eric F. Mason and Kevin B. McCruden. Atlanta: Society of Biblical Literature, 2011, pp. 13–29.

Gregory of Nyssa, *The Life of Moses.* Translation, introduction and notes by Everett Ferguson and Abraham J. Malherbe. Classics of Western Spirituality (New York: Paulist Press, 1978)

Gutiérrez, Gustavo. *We Drink from Our Own Wells: The Spiritual Journey of a People.* Translated by Matthew J. O'Connell. Maryknoll, NY: Orbis, 1985.

Hartin, Patrick J. *Exploring the Spirituality of the Gospels.* Collegeville, MN: Liturgical Press, 2010.

Hays, Richard B. *The Faith of Jesus Christ: An Investigation of the Narrative Substructure of Gal 31-4:11.* 2nd ed. Grand Rapids: Eerdmans, 2002.

Herzog, William R., II. *Prophet and Teacher: An Introduction to the Historical Jesus.* Louisville: Westminster John Knox, 2005.

Hilhorst, Anthony. "Abel's Speaking in Hebrews 11:4 and 12:24." In *Eve's Children: The Biblical Stories Retold and Interpreted in Jewish and Christian Traditions.* Themes in Biblical Narrative 5. Edited by Gerhard P.Luttikhuizen. Leiden: Brill, 2003, pp. 119–27.

Isaacs, Marie E. *Sacred Space: An Approach to the Theology of the Epistle to the Hebrews.* Journal for the Study of the New Testament Supplement Series 73. Sheffield: Sheffield Academic, 1992.

Johnsson, William G. "The Pilgrimage Motif in the Book of Hebrews." *Journal of Biblical Literature* 97 (1978): 239–51.

Johnson, Luke Timothy. *Among the Gentiles: Greco-Roman Religion and Christianity.* New Haven, CT: Yale University, 2009.

———. *Faith's Freedom: A Classic Spirituality for Contemporary Christians.* Minneapolis: Fortress Press, 1991.

———. *Hebrews: A Commentary.* New Testament Library. Louisville: Westminster John Knox Press, 2006.

Joseph, Abson Prédestin. *A Narratological Reading of 1 Peter.* Library of New Testament Studies 440. London: T & T Clark, 2012

Käsemann, Ernst. *The Wandering People of God: An Investigation of the Letter to the Hebrews.* Translated by R. A. Harrisville and I. L. Sandberg. Minneapolis: Augburg, 1984.

Koester, Craig R. *Hebrews: A New Translation with Introduction and Commentary.* Anchor Bible Commentary 36. New York: Doubleday, 2001.

Lane, William L. *Hebrews.* 2 vols. Word Biblical Commentary 47. Waco, TX: Word, 1991.

Lindars, Barnabas. *The Theology of the Letter to the Hebrews.* New Testament Theology. Cambridge: Cambridge University Press, 1991.

Lohr, Joel N. "Righteous Abel, Wicked Cain: Genesis 4:1-6 in the Masoretic Text, the Septuagint, and The New Testament." *Catholic Biblical Quarterly* 71 (2009): 485–96.

Matera, Frank J. "The Theology of the Epistle to the Hebrews." In *Reading the Epistle to the Hebrews: A Resource for Students*. Society of Biblical Literature Resources for Biblical Study 66. Edited by Eric F. Mason and Kevin B. McCruden. Atlanta: Society of Biblical Literature, 2011, pp. 189–208.

Malbon, Elizabeth Stuthers. *Hearing Mark: A Listener's Guide*. Harrisburg: Trinity Press, 2002.

Mason, Eric F. "Cosmology, Messianism, and Melchizedek." In *Reading the Epistle to the Hebrews: A Resource for Students*. Society of Biblical Literature Resources for Biblical Study 66. Edited by Eric F. Mason and Kevin B. McCruden. Atlanta: Society of Biblical Literature, 2011, pp. 53–76.

McCruden, Kevin B. "The Concept of Perfection in the Epistle to the Hebrews." In *Reading the Epistle to the Hebrews: A Resource for Students*. Society of Biblical Literature Resources for Biblical Study 66. Edited by Eric F. Mason and Kevin B. McCruden. Atlanta: Society of Biblical Literature, 2011, pp. 209–29.

———. *Solidarity Perfected: Beneficent Christology in the Epistle to the Hebrews*. Beihefte zur Zeitschrift für die neutestamentliche Wissenschaft 159. Berlin/New York: de Gruyter, 2008.

———. "Compassionate Soteriology in Mark, 1 Peter, and Hebrews." *Biblical Research* 52 (2007): 41–56.

———. "Judgment and Life for the Lord: Occasion and Theology of Romans 14, 1–15, 13." *Biblica* 86 (2005): 229–44.

———. "Christ's Perfection in Hebrews: Divine Beneficence as an Exegetical Key to Hebrews 2:10." *Biblical Research* 47 (2002): 40–62.

Mitchell, Alan C. *Hebrews*. Sacra Pagina 13. Collegeville, MN: Liturgical Press, 2007.

———. "A Sacrifice of Praise: Does Hebrews Promote Supersessionism?" In *Reading the Epistle to the Hebrews: A Resource for Students*. Society of Biblical Literature Resources for Biblical Study 66. Edited by Eric F. Mason and Kevin B. McCruden. Atlanta: Society of Biblical Literature, 2011, pp. 251–67.

Miller, James C. "Paul and Hebrews: A Comparison of Narrative Worlds." In *Hebrews: Contemporary Methods—New Insights*. Biblical Interpretation Series 75. Edited by Gabriela Gelardini. Leiden: Brill, Repr., Atlanta: Society of Biblical Literature, 2008.

Moberly, R. Walter L. "Exemplars of Faith in Hebrews 11: Abel." In *The Epistle to the Hebrews and Christian Theology*. Edited by Richard Bauckham, Daniel R. Driver, Trevor A. Hart, Nathan MacDonald. Grand Rapids: Eerdmans, 2009, pp. 353–63.

Moffatt, James. *A Critical and Exegetical Commentary on the Epistle to the Hebrews.* ICC. Edinburgh: T & T Clark, 1924.

Moffitt, David M. "Unveiling Jesus' Flesh: A Fresh Assessment of the Relationship between the Veil and Jesus' Flesh in Hebrews 10:20." In *Perspectives in Religious Studies* 37 (2010): 71–84.

———. *Atonement and the Logic of Resurrection in the Epistle to the Hebrews.* Supplementsto Novum Testamentum 141. Leiden: Brill, 2011.

Montifiore, Hugh. *The Epistle to the Hebrews.* Harper's New Testament Commentaries. New York: Harper & Row, 1984.

Najman, Hindy. "Cain and Abel as Character Traits: A Study in the Allegorical Typology of Philo of Alexandria." In *Eve's Children: The Biblical Stories Retold and Interpreted in Jewish and Christian Traditions.* Edited by Gerald P. Luttikhuizen. Leiden: Brill, 2003, pp. 107–18.

O'Brien, Peter T. *The Letter to the Hebrews.* Grand Rapids: Eerdmans, 2010.

Palmer, Parker J. *To Know as We Are Known: Education as a Spiritual Journey.* San Francisco: Harper, 1993.

Pascuzzi, Maria. "Baptism-based Allegiance and the Divisions in Corinth: A Reexamination of 1 Corinthians 1:13-17." *Catholic Biblical Quarterly* 71 (2009): 813–29.

Principe, Walter. "Toward Defining Spirituality." *Sciences Religieuses/Studies in Religion* 12, no. 2 (1983): 127–41.

Pursiful, Darrell. *The Cultic Motif in the Spirituality of the Book of Hebrews.* Lewiston: Edwin Mellen Press, 1993.

Rothschild, Clare K. *Hebrews as Pseudepigraphan: The History and Significance of the Pauline Attribution of Hebrews.* Wissenshaftliche Untersuchungen zum Neuen Testament 235. Tübingen: Mohr Siebeck, 2009.

Salevao, Iutisone. *Legitimation in the Letter to the Hebrews: The Construction and Maintenance of a Symbolic Universe.* Journal for the Study of the New Testament Supplement Series 219. London: Sheffield, 2002.

Schenck, Kenneth. *Cosmology and Eschatology in Hebrews: The Settings of the Sacrifice.* Society for New Testament Studies Monograph Series 143. Cambridge: Cambridge University Press, 2007.

———. *Understanding the Book of Hebrews: The Story Behind the Sermon.* Louisville: Westminster John Knox Press, 2003.

Schneiders, Sandra M. *The Revelatory Text: Interpreting the New Testament as Sacred Scripture*. San Francisco: Harper, 1991.

———. "The Study of Christian Spirituality: Contours and Dynamics of a Discipline." In *Minding the Spirit. The Study of Christian Spirituality*. Edited by Elizabeth A. Dreyer and Mark S. Burrows. Baltimore: Johns Hopkins, 2004.

Scholer, John M. *Proleptic Priests: Priesthood in the Epistle to the Hebrews*. Journal for the Study of the New Testament Supplement Series 49. Sheffield: Sheffield Academic, 1991.

Sheldrake, Philip. *A Brief History of Spirituality*. London: Wiley-Blackwell, 2007.

Sobrino, Jon. *Christ the Liberator: A View from the Victims*. Translated by Paul Burns. Maryknoll, NY: Orbis, 2001.

Spicq, Ceslas. *L'Epître aux Hébreux*. 2 vols. Paris: Gabalda, 1952–53.

Stendahl, Krister. *Paul among Jews and Gentiles*. Minneapolis: Fortress Press, 1976.

Stowers, Stanley K. *A Rereading of Romans: Justice, Jews, and Gentiles*. New Haven: Yale University Press, 1994.

Thatcher, Tom. "Cain and Abel in Early Christian Memory: A Case Study in the Use of the Old Testament in the New." *Catholic Biblical Quarterly* 72 (2010): 732–51.

Thompson, James W. *The Beginnings of Christian Philosophy: The Epistle to the Hebrews*. Catholic Biblical Quarterly Monograph Series 13. Washington, DC: Catholic Biblical Association, 1982.

———. "The New Is Better: A Neglected Aspect of the Hermeneutics of Hebrews." *Catholic Biblical Quarterly* 73 (2011): 547–61.

Tobin, Thomas H., SJ. *The Spirituality of Paul*. Eugene, OR: Wipf and Stock, 2008.

Westcott, Brooke Foss. *The Epistle to the Hebrews: The Greek Text with Notes and Essays*. London: Macmillan, 1892.

Wray, Judith Hoch. *Rest as a Theological Metaphor in the Epistle to the Hebrews and the Gospel of Truth: Early Christian Homiletics of Rest*. Society of Biblical Literature Dissertation Series 166. Atlanta: Scholars Press, 1998.

Index of Ancient Sources

Index of Persons and Subjects